SALVIA
DIVINORUM

"Fascinating. *Salvia Divinorum* is a clear, inspiring, and insightful account of meetings with a powerful teacher plant. In the spirit of the classical psychedelic explorers, J. D. Arthur kept a meticulous record of his work with *Salvia divinorum*. In this easy-to-read book he provides others with a road map for their own explorations, as well as a detailed guide to the territory. After reading Arthur's book I am inspired to look again at salvia."

ROSS HEAVEN, AUTHOR OF
PLANT SPIRIT SHAMANISM AND
THE HUMMINGBIRD'S JOURNEY TO GOD

SALVIA DIVINORUM

DOORWAY TO THOUGHT-FREE AWARENESS

J. D. ARTHUR

Park Street Press

Rochester, Vermont • Toronto, Canada

Park Street Press
One Park Street
Rochester, Vermont 05767
www.ParkStPress.com

Park Street Press is a division of Inner Traditions International

Note to the reader: *This book is intended as an informational guide. The approaches and techniques described herein should not be used by anyone with a history of mental illness or to treat a serious ailment.*

Library of Congress Cataloging-in-Publication Data

Arthur, J. D. (James Arthur)
  Salvia divinorum : doorway to thought-free awareness / J.D. Arthur.
      p. ; cm.
  Originally published as: Peopled darkness / J.D. Arthur. iUniverse. c2008.
  ISBN 978-1-59477-347-1 (pbk.)
  1. Salvia divinorum. 2. Hallucinations and illusions. I. Arthur, J. D. (James Arthur) Peopled darkness. II. Title.
  [DNLM: 1. Hallucinogens—Personal Narratives. 2. Salvia—Personal Narratives. 3. Awareness—Personal Narratives. QV 77.7 A788s 2010]
  RM324.8.A78 2010
  615'.7883—dc22

                                                        2009045797

Printed and bound in the United States

10   9   8   7   6   5   4

Text design and layout by Virginia Scott Bowman
This book was typeset in Garamond Premiere Pro and Legacy Sans with Bauer Text Initials and Gil Sans as display typefaces

To send correspondence to the author of this book, mail a first-class letter to the author c/o Inner Traditions • Bear & Company, One Park Street, Rochester, VT 05767, and we will forward the communication.

Special thanks to Daniel Siebert
for his encouragement.

CONTENTS

A NOTE TO THE READER

ON THE USE OF
SALVIA DIVINORUM

Salvia divinorum is a fairly recent addition to the visionary pharmacopoeia of the modern world. As such, it offers unexplored benefits, as well as dangers. The long-term consequences, both physical and psychological, of the ingestion of salvia and its concentrated extracts are, as yet, unknown. This, of course, doesn't imply that there are any adverse effects in the long run, but does indicate that one should proceed with caution, and that these unknown elements must be factored into any mature assessment of salvia's ultimate safety.

The experience of salvia ingestion is not necessarily a pleasant one. Many people have tried it once or twice and sworn off. In all probability, salvia will never be a popular pursuit. The disorienting nature of the trance is not the type of experience that people generally find entertaining.

These writings are in no way meant to encourage the use of salvia—to do so would be irresponsible. Although salvia is a legal visionary plant in most of the United States at this writing, many states have wisely limited its purchase and use to those over eighteen years of age. Unfortunately, some states as well as countries have banned its use altogether. Before considering any experimentation with salvia, one should check its legal status in one's state (or country, if outside the United States) to make sure no laws are being broken.*

The fact that much salvia experimentation occurs among younger people is disturbing. While salvia can be a valuable adjunct to sincere analysis of one's own perceptual relationship to the world at large, it also can be a source of disorienting delusion for those unequipped, due to the poverty of their life experience, to approach it with the proper balance of respect and skepticism. It should, therefore, never be used by those under the age of eighteen.

Due to the sometimes bizarre and overwhelming effects of salvia, those with any history of mental health issues should also avoid it.

---

*An excellent resource for the latest information on the legal status of salvia is the *Salvia divinorum* Research and Information Center (www.sagewisdom.org/legal status).

The future legality of salvia on a national level is still unknown at this time, but based on our general cultural view of genuine visionary pursuit, salvia will no doubt go the way of other mind-altering plants.

INTRODUCTION

I n the fall of 1962, two aging gentlemen, sitting on crude wooden saddles, rode on donkeys through the mountains of Oaxaca, Mexico. Their journey, arduous by any standards, was undertaken for one reason: they were in search of a treasure. The surroundings they encountered, though often beautiful, were daunting at times, and their travels were not without peril, but they were on a quest.

One of the two men was the renowned chemist Albert Hofmann, whose experimental work had led to the discovery of LSD-25. His companion, R. Gordon Wasson, was the author and amateur ethnobotanist who, years earlier, was instrumental in revealing the mystery of Teonanácatl, the Mexican hallucinogenic mushrooms, to the modern world. The treasure that drew them to these mountains was the elusive plant known as *Salvia divinorum*. The plant had been used for centuries by the Mazatecs for healing and divination, particularly when the sacred mushrooms were not in season. Along with the mushrooms and the hallucinogenic morning glory seeds, Ololiuqui, salvia completed the triad of plant allies so valued by the *curanderos.**

After finally locating samples of the legendary plant, as well as ingesting a preparation of its leaves under the guidance of a *curandera* during a divinatory ceremony, they succeeded in bringing back the first specimens for identification to arrive in the United States. Within months, other researchers—Sterling Bunnell, accompanied by poet Michael McClure—journeyed to the same areas in Mexico, this time retrieving live plants that would later be propagated, with samples eventually spreading to many parts of the world, thus offering, for the first time, a newly unearthed doorway that would open into the unknown.

In years to come, salvia's unique psychoactive component, salvinorin A, would be identified by the pioneering researcher Daniel Siebert, who would be the first to unravel the mysteries of its absorption through diverse preparations, as well as to delineate the mechanism of the various forms of ingestion.

With time, others would follow in their footsteps, providing additional genetic varieties and enlarging the scope of knowledge about salvia, while attracting adherents

---

*The traditional shamanic folk healers of Mexico and Central and South America.

throughout the world and assuring salvia a prominent place in the hierarchy of hallucinogenic plants.

The following account is a record of my personal experiences ingesting that same visionary plant over a period of several years. These are, of course, subjective experiences. This journal is not meant to either encourage or discourage anyone from exploring the effects of this plant for themselves. There is no implicit suggestion that these types of results are either accessible or inaccessible to others who might decide to experiment. People who explore such avenues will have their own motives, expectations, and predispositions, and no sweeping generalizations could or should be ventured. It is my personal belief that the perceptual transition herein described could be duplicated and surpassed by others of like mind.

To accept the following journal of experiences as true, without one's own experimentation and possible validation, would be counter to the spirit in which they were recorded. The experiential nature of visionary exploration is in itself a counterbalance to the all too common mode of "faith" that often seems to aim toward the limiting rather than toward the expansion of awareness.

To reject the following account based on skepticism is understandable. I myself would have considered much of it as either nonsense or delusion, had I come across it under different circumstances; and were it not for the relative ease of personal verification of many of the psychological states engendered by salvia, this would probably be the most rational conclusion one might reach.

The events described, although often quite remarkable in themselves, were not the ultimate transformative mechanism; rather, the changes that took place in my own perception, essentially redefining the identity of the perceiver, continue to hold the most significance. Regardless of the visions encountered, certain undeniable characteristics of perception and mentation have become apparent and have been uniquely pivotal in altering the way the world is subsequently viewed.

I've tried to avoid reading any meaning into the occurrences that unfolded, but have endeavored to report an accurate account of both the events witnessed as well as any resultant psychological responses or changes that could be relevant. When speculation has surfaced, it's been in the interest of communicating some of the more subtle feelings that would have been irretrievable by any other means.

No doubt, some contradictions can be found in my description, or interpretation, of some of the events described. These contradictions are the result of my portrayal rather than the states themselves, which always had an inner consistency and stability at their core. In many instances, the salient details of the visions were extremely vivid and seemed so palpable as to lend themselves easily to recounting. At other times, the nature of the occurrences was of such an abstract character that any attempt at recollection, much less description, seemed insurmountable.

In some instances, the chronology of specific occurrences was altered in order to clarify certain psychological nuances, or experiential similarities, that would thread through many trials. In general, though, the sequence of events was as portrayed. In many instances, I included which form of salvia was used as well as any other relevant information I might have recorded, in the event that it might be of interest to other experimenters.

Any philosophical implications arising from my experiences with salvia concerning the landscapes encountered, or the personages that people those landscapes, for example, have been beyond my control and would never have been my intention. Salvia did not fulfill any of my personal philosophical predispositions but, rather, devastated them. The touchstones that had served to define my concept of reality have had to be discarded, and a completely new set of reference points installed in their stead. What I might have viewed, previously, as theoretical philosophical posits revealed themselves as undeniable psychological verities through a level of awareness that was as unexpected as it was profound. Salvia forced me to reexamine an entire complex of perceptions and assumptions that, under normal circumstances, would have been safely immune from such scrutiny.

When including passages from my notes, I endeavored to reproduce the notes as accurately as possible to communicate the immediacy of many of the occurrences. If any changes were made, it was only to make more understandable what appeared, at times, as an incomprehensible chain of scrawled phrases. Any speculation within the text of the notes, I felt, was, on occasion, permissible, since it was guided by, and often retained the flavor of, the still recent experiences.

I chose not to include information concerning salvia's history, botany, and so forth because this information is so readily available from other, more knowledgeable sources. Without doubt, the best resource for all salvia information is the *Salvia divinorum* Research and Information Center run by Daniel Siebert (www.sagewisdom.org). The center's FAQ and User's Guide provide excellent background on the many facets of salvia.

Rather than repeat what research exists elsewhere, I wanted to provide a more experiential perspective, taking place over the course of time. This perspective has been lacking in the available literature, and I felt that the nature of the landscape I was exploring revealed unique details that I hadn't encountered in any other writings on salvia.

I

FIRST EXPERIENCES

*The greatest blessings come
by way of madness.*

SOCRATES

I n the summer of 2002, I began experimenting with
the visionary plant known as *Salvia divinorum,* or
diviner's sage. A member of the mint family, salvia
is also known by various names often associated in indigenous cultures with the Virgin Mary, such as "leaves of
the shepherdess" or "yerba Maria." It had been used for
centuries by the Mazatec Indians of Oaxaca, Mexico, for
healing, divination, and similar uses, when the sacred
hallucinogenic mushrooms were unavailable, and was
beginning to gain popularity among a growing subcul-
ture of experimenters who were using the plant and its

various preparations for spiritual or meditative pursuits.

Due to this growing interest, the plant was also becoming more readily available, as well as information regarding its use, effects, cultivation, and history.

Traditional ingestion of the plant consisted in chewing or eating a quid of the rolled-up leaves or drinking the expressed juice of dozens of crushed leaves. This method was reported to induce visions and facilitate contact with the plant spirit—some curanderos even claiming to speak with God and the saints. In recent years, particularly outside the traditional framework, smoking the dried, crushed leaves, as well as ingestion through a tincture, have been the most popular methods for approaching salvia.

According to published accounts, salvia seemed safe enough, and the experience, depending on the form of ingestion, was reported to last between five and thirty minutes. I had used LSD fairly often in the past and felt reasonably comfortable with hallucinogenic states. Even if the experience was unpleasant, I reasoned, it would be short lived. The fact that the plant had a shamanic legacy among native people added to my interest.

The active ingredient in salvia is salvinorin A, the concentration of which can vary significantly from plant to plant, based on heredity, growing conditions, and the like. Salvinorin A can, however, be extracted from the plant by the use of various solvents, such as acetone or ethanol. After evaporation of the solvent, the resultant salvinorin

A–rich precipitate can be redissolved into a tincture or redeposited on crushed leaves. Depending on the amount of salvinorin A extracted, the "enhanced" leaves normally vary in strength from 5X to 20X the original potency; although, in recent years, extracts as high as 60X have been sold.

The strength of salvia seemed to be somewhat of an issue because many claimed to have horrific, disorienting experiences. It seemed that, in many cases, these same people were using very strong extracts of the plant, if not pure salvinorin A itself. In some published accounts, salvia was used in addition to other powerful substances such as LSD and DMT. Finding information about the effects of lighter, more rational doses of salvia was more elusive.

After some research, I decided to begin with the liquid tincture. It seemed, first of all, the mildest approach, as well as slightly longer lasting than smoking. It also seemed to be the method of ingestion most similar in effect to the indigenous methods used by the Mazatecs.

Although they would either drink the juice or chew the leaves, their method, I was given to understand, seemed to rely on absorption through the oral mucosa, which was the same as the tincture. The amount of leaves, by many accounts, that would be needed for something approaching traditional methods would also be prohibitive.

The procedure was to hold a measured amount of the tincture in the mouth, preferably under the tongue, for a specified amount of time without swallowing. This would allow the dissolved salvinorin A to enter the blood-stream though the tissues of the mouth. This can get a bit problematic, since the mouth tends to generate saliva as a response to the mildly burning tincture, and the urge to swallow increases. I would use the equivalent of six or eight eyedroppers full for about twelve minutes.

In addition to the fact that I lived in a very rural area, I was fortunate to have a small workshop near my house that would afford me silence and solitude for any exploration. I wanted to adhere, as closely as possible, to the traditional recommendations for salvia use. To that end, I would use total darkness, as well as closed eyes, for my approach. These conditions of isolation virtually eliminated any visual or aural distraction or grounding influences of ordinary stimuli and allowed me to uninter-ruptedly let go and abandon myself to any circumstances that might arise. Although it was advised to always have a "sitter" present during these explorations, I personally felt that the solitude would be more beneficial, especially since I planned on smaller, safer doses to start. I was later to amend this decision for other reasons that I'll relate subsequently.

My first experience, although interesting, was fairly uneventful. The nature of the images that presented themselves was unlike the images that I'd come to expect from other hallucinogens such as LSD or peyote. These images were more elusive and fragmented. My experiences with LSD would generally be accompanied by harmonious unfolding of seemingly infinite geometric relationships, ringing with emotional, if not spiritual, overtones.

These salvia-induced images were different. They seemed at first to be almost without feeling—random and confused. There might be a fleeting image of a tortured facial expression, followed by a sensation of a tearing, sliding movement. There could be a seemingly arbitrary phrase that might present itself just beneath hearing, the way a fragment of a tune might make itself heard in an almost unconscious manner.

During these trials, I never felt overwhelmed by the experience and never lost touch with consensual reality. I felt that at any point I could open my eyes and stand up, essentially dispelling the visions that were, though palpable, tenuous. One thing, however, seemed a bit different with salvia. From my first experiences, there was a strange, underlying sense of what I can only describe as "presences." It was as if, on some level, I was not alone. There seemed to be a surrounding aura of what might be termed "personalness," which was oddly comforting despite its foreignness. At first, it emerged as a feeling of being hurried, as if someone were waiting for me while I held the tincture in my mouth. This was an odd feeling, since there was no reason for haste. I thought that it was perhaps a reaction to timing myself for the duration of the twelve minutes. As time went on, however, it began to feel as if there were actually people awaiting my "arrival." During this time, I never "saw" anyone; rather, my visitors were more in the realm of feeling on a level that was just below the threshold of awareness.

Aside from this vague feeling of presence, my experiences during this time were generally unremarkable. My initial impression was that salvia seemed to portray an odd randomness, exhibiting visions that seemed somehow precise, yet arbitrary. There was an occasional fleeting vignette that might pique my interest, but, in general, it seemed that something more was needed to initiate any palpable change of consciousness. It seemed that the time had come to begin experimenting with the stronger effects of smoked salvia. I decided to begin with the unenhanced dried salvia leaves. This was the first logical step up from the tincture. It also seemed, unlike the stronger extracts, to be more controllable.

When smoking salvia, there is a definite procedure to be followed in order to best experience the effects. First of all, one wants to fill the lungs as fully as possible with the smoke; therefore, a pipe is preferable to a rolled cigarette. Due to the harshness of the smoke, some people prefer water pipes to cool and filter the resultant smoke. I, personally, found that a corncob pipe worked perfectly. In addition, one could have two or three pipes loaded with salvia before smoking, thus multiple lungfuls could be taken sequentially, without the necessity for reloading while one is in a semi-inebriated state. Secondly, due to the high vaporization temperature, as well as safety concerns, an ordinary disposable butane lighter is well suited to ignite the salvia, the flame being held continuously over the bowl of the pipe. Lastly, the smoke must be retained in the lungs for as long as possible. This, obviously, aids in the absorption of the smoke by the lung tissue.

My first experience with smoked salvia was of a decidedly different order than with the tincture. Whereas the tincture allowed one the luxury of "snapping out" of the experience, the smoked salvia was more demanding and disorienting. The visions were more intense and involving, although still retaining their arbitrary nature.

Smoked salvia was anything but pleasant. The vignettes could range from the mundane to the nauseatingly bizarre. Again there were presences, but more nagging and disorienting. The visions, in my case, were meaningless, repulsive images from the '40s and '50s. Cartoon characters, crooning trios from the '40s, roller-skating carhops—all made their appearance in a maddening swirl of nonsense.

To make matters worse, it became apparent that this was not a controllable situation. I was being sucked into this cacophonous vortex, while trying desperately to hold on to my sanity. Thankfully, the experience was fairly short lived, lasting only four or five minutes, but leaving me with a profound sense of relief that I had escaped this whirl of madness unscathed. For the first time in my life, I'd felt that my mind was no longer under my command and that the power to control such a state was beyond my grasp.

Salvia was unlike any other mind-altering substance I'd ever experienced. Besides its frightening grasp on the mind, it also seemed devoid of the types of emotional richness I'd experienced with hallucinogens in the past. How could absurd visions of roller-skating carhops possibly be of any use for spiritual exploration? The visions themselves seemed odd, since I had no choice but to conclude that they were images from some deep, unknown region of my own psyche; their arbitrary, cartoonish nature seemed foreign to my own life and actually felt as if they were being "presented" to me, rather than being revealed from within some part of myself.

The whole experience was actually a disappointment. I'd felt that I'd finally gotten my hands on a genuine divinatory plant, used for centuries by the native peoples of Mexico, and the best my demented Western psyche could come up with was this freakish cartoon. I felt that my newfound enthusiasm for salvia had come to a screeching halt. I decided at the time that I should try it once more, just to make sure. I thought the chances were likely that, after one or two more sessions, I'd abandon salvia as a pointless deliriant.

About a week later, I decided to smoke again. I loaded

two pipes with Mazatecan leaf, as I'd done previously. I was expecting another plunge into madness and had no expectations. After smoking, I began feeling the same disorientation—the same feeling of fighting for control; I began to see, as well as feel, the same '50s motif—the same cartoonish images.

This time, however, something was just slightly different. It seemed as if there were some type of link with my last excursion. It was as if, rather than starting out with a new series of inexplicable images, I was somehow picking up where I'd left off. There was an odd sense of continuation. There seemed to be something interesting about the experience this time—it felt a bit less threatening, less foreign. There was almost an element of humor, as if I were being told that I didn't need to be taking things so seriously. There were also, on some level that was totally unknown to me, various images that seemed to parody my holding on to the ordinary world. The mechanism of this parody eludes description; it was more like a complex of feelings reminiscent of the fever dreams that claim one's mind during illness than an actual scene viewed with the eyes. This, in itself, was an interesting phenomenon. It was almost as if I were being chided, on some level, for my state of mind.

Although this seemed to be an odd development, it didn't seem that significant at the time; it was merely another oddity connected with salvia. It is only in retrospect that the situation held some significance.

After returning to normal awareness, I noticed that the effects of salvia would linger for about an hour. This was, at the time, another interesting development. In the past, after a hallucinogenic experience such as LSD, the "after-glow" state was a very enjoyable transition. Everything appeared in a new and meaningful light that one would endeavor to savor and prolong.

Salvia, on the other hand, was a different experience for me. The ordinary world was a relief. After the induced "madness" of salvia, the mundane elements of normal life were a restful balm. It was as if the salviaic experience was so disturbing, at such a depth, that any distraction was welcome and refreshing. Although this characterization of the salvia experience can appear to weigh heavily on the negative side, there was, at the same time, a growing excitement fueled by the all-encompassing reality of the experience. I'd never come across anything like this before. The short time that one is actually in the salviaic state is, in the beginning at least, a merciful benefit. I remember thinking, at the time, that if the experience lasted much longer, the prolonged intensity would be psychologically devastating.

I continued smoking salvia at irregular intervals throughout the following months. Again, my experiences were beginning to evince some sort of internal consistency. The nature of the images and feelings I would encounter were always changing, but there seemed to be developing what might be called a cumulative awareness. Somehow, there seemed to be a continuity among the successive forays. They were frightening on the one hand, but somehow fascinating on the other. The more I entered this state, the more I was becoming familiar with this terrifying foreignness.

During this time, it was becoming apparent that, despite the fear and apprehension accompanying each event, one thing was obvious—I'd always come back—my mind was still intact. However disorienting the experience, it was, indeed, temporary. I was feeling more and more confident that nothing bad would happen to me "over there." At the same time, I was beginning to adapt to the state that had been so foreign initially. I was beginning to let go. The fear that I was losing my mind, in my first experiences with salvia, had loosened its grip a bit. I was unconsciously becoming more willing to relinquish, for a few moments, the fierce clinging to the psychological framework that defines and stabilizes the world. Of course, after returning, I wanted that same framework— rock solid and steady—once again, and it always was. Salvia was offering me the option to explore both sides.

My experiences with salvia during this time were radically different from one to the next, but I was beginning to notice certain similarities among the events. My usual procedure was to load two pipes with crushed dried salvia leaves. I'd then smoke both pipes in succession, although oftentimes, after holding and releasing the smoke from the first pipe, the effects would already be beginning to be felt. After exhaling the last pipeful, the full effects would begin.

Most times the journey would be initiated by a centering of the visual field. It was as if I'd become aware of a central point in my field of view that would somehow unfold and spew out a rush of images and feelings. The images themselves were very much like dream images— vague and shadowy, yet wholly present. In my case, there would be a splash of rushing faces—peripherally demanding—occasionally voicing words or performing actions in a fleeting sequence that was as vague as it was ephemeral. This flood of faces would be accompanied by a wave of feelings that had a peculiar flavor. They were not the ordinary feelings of joy or fear, but would be imbued with a specific "foreignness." This would be apparent only later when the event was being recalled. What had seemed somehow understandable in the state was now irretrievably beyond reach.

On a somatic level, the experiences were all fairly similar. As the rush of faces and scenes would envelop me, my attention would be focused strongly on those elements, while, at the same time, my body would be in a state of what might be termed "tense repose." Salvia would have the dual effect of numbing the body, to a certain extent, in an external way, while at the same time engaging the bodily senses in a very direct, yet internal way. After first entering the state, I would feel something akin to "pins and needles"—primarily, it seemed, in my face. This gentle stinging was all but unnoticeable, initially. It always seemed intertwined with the psychological aspects of entering the state, as if the two were one process. It was not an unpleasant sensation; on the contrary, it was exhilarating. It was an almost blissful corollary to the dipping into the well of faces.

Another physical sensation that was regularly making its appearance was the overwhelming sensation of movement. Initially, there seemed to be a rapid forward movement, as if one were plunging headlong into a pool of water. The movement was swift and sustained. Within a few moments, I would become aware of secondary forces moving laterally to the left or right. This has been a consistent occurrence throughout many of my salvia journeys. There is a profound feeling of direction in many experiences. Oftentimes, I would feel that I was being blown by a strong "wind," to my left or right. It would become paramount to "hold on" and not be swept away. This wind would make its presence felt often in subsequent sessions, to a greater or lesser extent. Again, this was not an unpleasant experience necessarily but, rather, part of the all-encompassing landscape that was gradually opening before me.

This sensation of direction was evidently so involving that I would often "awaken" with my head turned strongly to the left, almost over my shoulder. I'd been totally unaware that such physical correlates had been in play. These were the only instances, however, where there was any type of physical counterpart to the intense inner forces that were claiming my attention.

In addition to the sensation of movement, which was becoming a regular feature of my experiences, was the feeling that I was pushing upward through some sort of membrane at the crown of my head. The image that presented itself was not unlike a cocoon from which I was emerging. Like so many of the experiences unique to the state of salvia "intoxication," it seemed remarkably natural and somehow familiar. The sensation was, on some level, almost what one might term "organically instructive," while at the same time was physically approaching what one might call a "state of bliss."

The intensity of this occurrence would vary, but it would come to be a regular feature of many experiences. Often, after I returned to the normal state, the crown of my head, seemingly at the point of the crown chakra in Hindu physiology, would be sore, although this was not a particularly unpleasant sensation. I mention the crown chakra not to draw any inference but merely to more precisely isolate the location of the sensation.

During this time, the experiences I was having began

to take on more of what might be termed "personal" characteristics. I was becoming accustomed to interactions, on some level, with "others." These interactions would usually consist of short vignettes often accompanied by some type of verbal description or injunction. Often these declarations would be in response to a question that was never asked. For instance, on one occasion, I was instructed to, "Tell her (my wife E. was implied) you're with us." At the same time, I found myself surrounded by vaguely familiar dolphinlike beings, who seemed to exude a playful joy.

There was a brief but vivid sensation of exuberant swimming. Again, this episode was, although very brief, emotionally significant; the event left me with the impression that, although alien, this world could also be welcoming and perhaps even protective.

This also was one of the first times I noticed a process that would repeat itself often in the future: the manner in which one asked a question. Here, a question is a verbal formation consisting of a sequence of words coupled with an interrogatory word or phrase. Over there, a question seems to consist of a state of feeling or being. One doesn't have to voice a question; indeed, it appears that one might not even know that one is asking a question—it's simply a state. Only after receiving an answer does one intuit that a question must have been asked. One could posit that this state of questioning might be accomplished by consciously or unconsciously holding a specific person or thought in mind, but I've felt that this was most often not the case, since the answers given would be in response to something well outside my normal frame of reference.

It was during this time I began experimenting with a stronger form of salvia known as 5X. This enhanced leaf contains approximately five times the salvinorin A content of regular crushed leaves, allowing one to consume considerably less smoke, while engendering a more powerful experience than could be achieved with normal crushed leaves. This enabled me to enter the state in a more immediate and forceful manner.

My first experiences with 5X were dramatic and exhilarating. The depth of the trance was stronger and more all encompassing than I'd experienced to date. The sensing of the presences was overwhelming. It was during this time I began to feel that the reality of genuine entities in this realm was undeniable. The depth and richness of this state was unlike anything I had ever encountered. On a physical level as well, I was beginning to experience sensations that were radically different from any I'd experienced previously. I began to feel the disturbing sensation that, with the slightest effort, I would be able to disconnect from my physical body.

This, like so many other facets of the salviaic experience, hinged on a unique series of perceptual events that, in their totality, gave rise to a singular mode of perceptual knowledge. This, seemingly very real, potential for leaving the body consisted of a physiological "acknowledgment" of a new series of somatic perceptions describing, in effect, a new "body." This new body could be intuited and on some level almost felt. This was experienced simultaneously with the abandonment of the usual sensations that define and reinforce the normal perception of the body. It was as if the perceptual bias of physicality could be altered by merely shifting the perceptual emphasis from one modality to the other. Salvia seemed to, on the one hand, minimize the normal physical sensations flowing from the body through its numbing effects, while at the same time enhancing these inner sensations through means that were as mysterious as they were palpable.

Although this sensation of the potential for leaving the body was somewhat frightening, it felt, once again, remarkably natural. Since all these sensations, as well as the world I was beginning to explore, were completely new to me—as well as intimations I was beginning to glean in consecutive salvia excursions—I opted not to abandon myself so readily to a sphere that was opening up so rapidly and was, to say the least, so incomprehensible.

In the months to come, this sensation—that I could abandon the normal physical matrix almost at will—became a regular feature of my experiences with salvia and seems to be the mechanism of many of the transformative processes that have made their appearance over the course of time.

2
INTENSIFICATION

I t was in this first year of experimentation that my experiences began to take on an increasing sense of realness that was both alarming and exhilarating. I was beginning to feel that I was becoming connected to a genuine "place" that entailed both psychological and physical dimensions.

During this period, I was also becoming increasingly familiar with this state and the inhabitants that were becoming the focus of these events. The fact that I would encounter these personages on a consistent basis was beginning to define the nature of the experience itself. I was feeling more of an emotional connection that was slowly, but decidedly, coming into focus. The vignettes that presented themselves were of a more personal nature than before, with more interaction from my companions. What had once manifested as a meaningless cacophony was gradually

becoming transformed into a coherent, approachable phenomenon. Although the entire course of the event was alien
and uncontrollable, there still remained an increasing interest in the connectedness that was gradually unfolding.

In order to remember as much as possible about the
experiences I was undergoing, I began to keep an occasional
journal detailing some of the more salient events. At the
time, I had mixed feelings about committing my experiences to paper. I thought that it might, on some level, be
antithetical to the genuine alien nature of these experiences,
which, by their very nature, could barely be recalled, much
less described accurately in words. It was as if I was afraid I
might jeopardize the flow of interaction I was experiencing
by focusing my ordinary awareness on the state. I thought
that, perhaps, I should simply experience these events and
not look back.

I also had no reason to believe that the successive trials
would entail any dramatic progression beyond what I was
already witnessing. To have a journal of consecutive incidents seemed an amusing, but arbitrary, waste of time. The
radical nature of the experiences I was having, coupled with
my wish to recount, as completely as possible, the nature of
these experiences with a few close friends, however, over-
came my reticence. Generally I would record my passages
on the day following the event, but after a period of time,
I began my recounting within an hour of returning to my
normal state. This tended to facilitate a more complete

retelling of the events, as well as to augment my memory with the still lingering flavor of the excursion.

One particular event during this initial period was especially vivid and can serve to illustrate the general tenor of my experiences at the time. From my notes:

———

One bowl 5X Mazatecan:

After smoking one bowl, the effects were instantaneous. Immediately, I saw a symmetrical flower, perhaps eight pointed, which opened into the other world, as I sensed the presence of beings, simultaneously. The immediacy of the change was startling. There was quite a bit of disorientation. I sensed that there was someone there. Suddenly, I encountered a male about forty or fifty years old with a black mustache. He appeared to be Mexican. It occurred to me that he might somehow be connected with the salvia I had just smoked—possibly a farmer or some sort of guardian of the plants. He was laughing good naturedly at my growing predicament—I could not remember who I was or from where I'd come.* I knew that I had another life somewhere but couldn't remember

———

*This loss of memory, apparently, came on very rapidly, since moments before, I'd been aware that I'd smoked salvia and what salvia was. I wasn't actually aware of the point at which this amnesic state began, but only when I attempted to recollect did I notice my dilemma.

anything about it. I couldn't remember whether I was an adult or a child and was quite disoriented.

Suddenly, a very raucous parade, complete with marching band, flags, and a bass drum engulfed me. This was also so bizarrely out of context that I felt even more bewildered. The parade came from my right. After a moment of horrifying confusion, I realized that the parade was a prank performed by an old man who also appeared off to my right. He was older than the first and very thin. He had evidently concocted the parade as a way of teasing me about my amnesic predicament.

Just then, two young girls entered the scene. They were about eleven years old, possibly twins, and were evidently daughters of the Mexican. They had black hair pulled back into buns and were wearing skirts and black shoes. They were also laughing, aware of my situation, and teasing me. One of them, as a way of describing my inability to remember where I was from, began joking. She said something, which on some level I found precise and hilarious, and I attempted to repeat what she had said. When I began to speak, I was unable to form the words. At the same time, I realized that it was a language that I couldn't speak. Evidently, to demonstrate my anxiety about my loss of memory, she leaped down and put her foot into a crevice in the floor—which was not flat, but looked organic, like a living being. I noticed that I was standing, perhaps ankle deep in this crevice, which was not unlike a huge vagina. This somehow was meant to demonstrate my predicament. They were all laughing good-naturedly at me, including the old man, who apparently was the uncle of the girls.

Shortly after this, the scene began to lose its intensity and slowly began to slip away. There was an image of a cloth slowly descending—as when someone is making a bed and the airborne sheet slowly comes to rest on the mattress. It was at this point that I began to remember who I was, along with some of the details of my other life.

During this time, similar vignettes would present themselves. I would find myself in circumstances that were at once foreign yet familiar. In all of these instances, I would be at a total loss as to who I was, how old I was, or from where I'd come. On some level, I was aware that I'd initiated some sort of action that had led me to that circumstance, but could not remember that it had been to smoke a hallucinogenic substance, or that I began the journey sitting in a chair in a small workshop. Although to focus on this amnesic state could lead to increasing panic, one could just as easily let go and simply perceive what was unfolding.

Indeed, it seems that this is one of the salient features of salvia—it allows one, in some sense even instructs one—to gradually, and without fear, abandon the framework of reason that's based on a cumbersome conceptual reference, and that is never called into question throughout the course of one's life. It's been my experience that salvia can lead to a unique state that one might characterize as "thoughtless awareness." This state, although on the surface seemingly paradoxical, is actually strangely and reassuringly familiar. It's as if, with repeated trances, one develops this skill gradually and effortlessly, leading to a genuine, what might be termed "functional awareness" that seems inherently essential for this type of exploration.

It was during this time that a particular episode occurred that, in retrospect, I hold significant, although at the time, I regarded as inconsequential. After smoking, I experienced the usual onset of images. Within a few moments, the state focused somewhat, and I found myself in the presence of an older woman. She was of slight build and seemed to be either Haitian or perhaps East Indian. She was wearing a long skirt and headscarf and seemed to be performing an odd action with her hands, as if she were drawing something apart or perhaps kneading and pulling an imaginary doughlike substance—it seemed reminiscent of playing the "cat's cradle" string game, only without the string. She had a bored demeanor and said, almost offhandedly, "You're accepted." On some level, it was implied that this was connected with a type of proficiency at "letting go," although these feelings were very vague. It was as if she, personally, couldn't care less about the information she was relaying—it seemed as though she was merely fulfilling a task. Within moments, the scene faded and I found myself returning to a normal state.

The next morning, I was initially hesitant to relate the story to E., since it would sound so pompous, while at the same time the experience itself had little or no emotional impact. I thought it was just another scene that was part of the flood of random images that I was encountering and thought no more about it. I didn't bother writing the experience down.

About a week later, I decided to smoke again. I followed my usual routine. This time, however, something was different. Even now, years later, it is difficult to pinpoint exactly what this difference entailed. Somehow, on some level, the state had stabilized. I was now returning to the same place, although this place did not necessarily entail location, in the normal sense. It was rather a state or feeling that had gained some sort of perceptual and emotional solidity. Although all the various external features of the visions were different, there was something that I was returning to—something was becoming familiar. In subsequent experiences, there would open up an entire range of feelings that was always somehow rooted in this abstract stable place.

During this time, my experiences involved a new range of emotions, that was often strangely comforting. I was beginning to feel a decided kinship with something with which I'd been totally unfamiliar. In one event, for instance, I was witnessing a scene that, externally, was insignificant. It was a small hut in a clearing. It was implied that there were other dwellings nearby, but they were outside my sphere of vision. The hut looked primitive but not recognizable as belonging to any particular time or culture. This scene, however, was accompanied by a group of feelings that were somehow a unified whole. These feelings encompassed peacefulness, a feeling of familial warmth, and a perception of what might be characterized as a sense of belonging to a tribal group. There were also overtones of a mode of simple, natural awareness that were somehow soothing. Like so many of my encounters in the salviaic state, this, once again, was alien yet curiously familiar. To say that these emotions felt as if they somehow echoed archaic memories would be to imply more than I intend, but they did seem to represent the ultimate fulfillment of some type of primordial human yearning.

There were also other instances, which would be repeated in varying degrees in subsequent trials, where I found myself the outsider. What tended to predominate in many of these sessions was the perception, occasionally voiced, that my presence was almost an inconvenience, an annoyance that was endured, for whatever reason. Often, this would result in a chiding or joking atmosphere. I was the burden that had to be borne, sometimes literally. On a few occasions, there was the perception that I was being carried, almost like a toddler.

In one session, I was being carried in some type of hammocklike sling that seemed to be made of some sort of netting. On another occasion, I found myself in a group of children (I also was a child) who were being taught by an older person. The teacher appeared displeased or annoyed by my presence. He was evidently persuaded to let me stay due to one or more of the students in the class. One peculiar aspect to this occurrence was the feeling that the teacher was used to dealing with "my type" and disliked the process. It was unclear at the time what characteristics delineated my type, but I felt that I was part of a group that was shunned for one reason or another. Interestingly, I came away from the experience with an odd feeling of kinship with my advocates.

It was also at this time that some of my experiences began to take on a somewhat disconcerting aspect. On several of my excursions, I was given to understand that the realm that I was exploring was connected with the dead. This was a somewhat shocking revelation; since it went against everything I would normally believe. I would usually consider any references to a simplistic concept such as the "land of the dead" as either allegory or superstitious babble. Nevertheless, my experiences were beginning to lead me in a different direction that I had no choice but to explore.

On one particular occasion, I had smoked two bowls of Oaxacan salvia. I was immediately taken, apparently under each arm by two young girls aged fourteen to sixteen. Not knowing my age, I had the distinct impression that they were older than I, not unlike big sisters. They were laughing and joking, moving me along as if they were escorting me somewhere. I was enlivened with feelings of joy and exhilaration. At one point the girl on my right suddenly recoiled, withdrawing her arm from mine. She seemed to be revolted by me. As she backed away she declared, "You're not dead!" in an accusatory fashion and withdrew. The feeling I experienced was that they had presumed that I was dead and was somehow joining them. As I began to regain an awareness of my surroundings, it seemed that the girls' revulsion stemmed from the fact that I had a flesh-and-blood body, which was evidently a disgusting concept to them.

As I began to settle into normal awareness, I had a fleeting memory of the previous time I had smoked. In that encounter, someone there, a male, had also said something to the effect of, "They're usually dead when they're here," but it seemed more of an impartial observation on his part, and not meant to impart anything of importance. Strangely, I had forgotten this vignette in the intervening time.

These references to the dead, or "land" or "place" of
the dead, would be repeated at intervals during the coming
months. Sometimes they would be in response to one of
the unvoiced questions. One woman who seemed almost
annoyed, asserted, "Of course, this is the land (or place) of
the dead!" as if it were obvious to anyone but a fool.

The presences I was encountering on a regular basis
were a paradoxical adjunct to my pursuits with salvia.
On the one hand, I had no idea who or what they were. I
felt that they were real enough to cause me harm, if they
wished. They never struck me as particularly benevolent—
neither did they seem threatening. On the other hand, I
was beginning to view aspects of their world with great
affection. I was beginning to trust the experience a bit.

When they first made their appearance, the word that
came to mind, in attempting to recall the encounter, was
spirit—not due to any specific attributes of theirs, but
more due to the poverty, not only of our language, but
also of our concepts. How else could they be described?
They weren't angels. They weren't devils. They weren't
spectral visages. They had all the attributes of ordinary
people. On one salvia excursion, this appellation had evidently been on my mind, on some level, while just entering the state. In that outer region, I might have been
anticipating encountering the spirits. It seemed that as I
entered the state and was beginning contact, the concept
of spirits seemed not only grossly inaccurate, but demean-

ing and disrespectful. Since that time I've preferred to characterize them as "presences," "companions," and the like, both from a wish for precision, as well as from a feeling of deference.

Evidently, one of the primary uses of salvia among the Mazatecs, as well as among some contemporary adherents, is in the area of divination. Since salvia seemed to have so many unknown possibilities, I thought it would be worth exploring this aspect as well. It was suggested in some recent writings that one should hold a question or similar thought in mind while entering the state. This would evidently focus the mind on a particular person or event, which would be elaborated upon by the salvia.

I smoked my usual amount of salvia while concentrating on a particular thought. As I began to enter the state, it became obvious that, in order to genuinely enter that realm to which I was becoming accustomed, I once again, in an ironic twist, would have to relinquish my ordinary thought processes, which, of course, was precisely where my question resided. Without the footing of thought, there could be no question. It just didn't seem possible to bring the camel with me through the eye of the needle. It was becoming obvious to me that the form of awareness that characterizes what I'd come to understand as the salviaic state was radically different from what we normally think of as "mentation." It's not so much that we are witnesses of perceptions brought on by salvia; rather, we, ourselves, change in our very nature, when entering the state. This change grants us access to a new range and quality of perceptions that would be impossible to grasp with our slow, lumbering, fragmented consciousness. The new awareness is immediate, fluid, and unencumbered with the bulky armor of conceptual thought.

As I went deeper into the state, other more subtle feelings surfaced. It seemed that to enter the state tenaciously holding on to a thought was rude, almost belligerent. One was entering a deep transcendent experience, and to carry in any conceptual baggage, as if to demand its validation, was a demonstration of disrespect. It was not that anyone or anything would be offended, rather, that the acquisition of this state of trance was the result of several factors, one of which, it seems, is a type of openness or humility. Of course, this was my own subjective assessment, and I don't mean to paint with too broad a brush. The particular state that I, myself, was entering necessitated these conclusions; it demanded a more or less total break with consensual reality.

Perhaps this is not always the case with others. To be aware of one's surroundings, people, and other images on a conscious level is a different state than the one to which I've been referring. I don't mean to imply that this type of experience isn't valid, it's simply not the one I found myself bound to pursue. Perhaps at some time in the future, this avenue of divination will seem somehow more accessible, possibly through some type of twilight state with which I'm as yet unfamiliar; but at present, I'm inclined to abandon its pursuit.

During this time, the intensity of my experiences would vary. Oftentimes, I would simply find myself in a scene that would engender simple groups of feelings. I would emerge in what felt like a type of kitchen, seated with a group of people. The scene itself was vague, but the feelings accompanying it were warm and welcoming. I felt a kinship with my hosts, and a sense of acceptance. On another occasion, I was being "dressed" or somehow prepared for some type of event or ceremony—again—feelings of affection and protection predominated.

At other times, the scenes were more intense and demanding. One such excursion occurred on a somewhat deeper level. I was in the process of lighting the second pipe when I began to feel all the effects of the first. I felt the presences impatiently hovering. My coordination seemed impaired, so I took a few token puffs and put the pipe down. I was getting acclimatized to the state, when suddenly it seemed as though a strong wind was blowing me irresistibly to the left, with great force. At the same time I distinctly heard a voice say, "Just come with us." There was an impatient tone to the suggestion. It was definitely more of the nature of a suggestion than a command. Although the pull was very strong, I was reluctant to let go completely and be swept away to something that was so totally unknown. I was able to maintain my hold; and although the urging seemed instructive and gentle, it seemed best to decline, particularly in light of recent allusions to the dead.

It seemed that this particular session was the most pronounced and immediate contact I'd experienced to date. This was the first time I'd felt such an emphatic and personal invitation from such an unknown source. This scenario would repeat itself quite often in the years to come. There is usually a group of people beckoning me in a genuinely friendly manner to join them. The state this appeal engenders is very paradoxical. On the one hand, it seems a magical opportunity, the possibilities of which seem limitless. On the other hand, one is gradually given to understand that death itself is a magical beckoning that holds endless promise as well. Whether these two states of invitation are one and the same is unknown. At this point, I've declined the invitations, since, to fully acquiesce, it would seem that one should be willing to accept equally the genuine possibility of either option.

Among other "fixed stars" that have shown some movement under salvia's influence has been the concept of time. Reason, from our normal perspective, would posit that the experience of salviaic trance is short lived and that one must always return. The power and intensity of the reality of the salvia state, however, would posit that time and reason are part of this world, not that world,

and that both realms are decidedly separate, if not antithetical to each other. The rules that apply in this world
don't apply there.

On a few occasions, I've had the feeling that there
were "pockets of eternity" into which one could slip and
be trapped. These feelings, of course, don't give validity of
themselves to this concept, but since one's mind, thoughts,
and language can all seem foreign and out of one's control,
these feelings can be daunting. The reality of this world is
based upon our evaluation and acceptance of the totality
of our sense perceptions. The reality of the salviaic state is
also based upon the same criteria, no matter how bizarre
or disconcerting those perceptions might be.

Since time itself is a concept resulting from perceptions of our physical body in this world, held together
with the glue of thought and memory, once these factors
are taken out of play, nothing is immune from transformation. It seems theoretically possible that, since time is
inexorably linked with perception, if the nature of those
perceptions is altered, the perception of time might also
be altered. If our linear perception of time is represented
by a horizontal line, the salviaic perception of time might
be seen as a vertical spike, varying in amplitude, in that
line. The aboriginal concept of "dream time" seems to
allude to such possibilities. Salvia can give the impression
of being outside time, since the factors that engender and
define the passage of time have been transformed. If, as

science tells us, time itself can be altered by such seemingly unrelated factors such as gravity and motion, perhaps other factors, of a more penetrating interior nature, should not be dismissed so readily. Ironically, time, it seems, needs a perceiver of its passage to exist.

Another area of psychological certitude that was beginning to strain under the weight of these increasingly bizarre impressions was the centering of the self in one's own body. One extremely frightening concept began to make its appearance during this time, as well as in many times subsequently. I was becoming more involved in the reality of my visions, while at the same time relinquishing all memory of my former self. It was as if I might actually "awaken" in one of these realms, with no memory to serve as a way of returning. This feeling that one could slip so easily to the other side is quite terrifying, yet is so common, that it seems intrinsic to the journey:

―――――

E. present. Very strong direct experience. Taken by presences—had the distinct feeling that I could "wake up" over there—in very ordinary circumstances. It seemed as if they were encouraging me to do so.

It was as if I could awaken over there and this world would be a dream that would fade. It appeared that I was seated there and was wearing some sort of white coat. There might have been a tile floor. There were myriad associations or facets of affection that I seemed to be rapidly experiencing—none specifically, it seemed, from this or that world: very commonplace feelings swiftly moving past my awareness.

Again there was a difference of language or, more specifically, a range of alien memories or associations, which were familiar on a very deep level, but were at the same time foreign to another part of myself. As I felt myself returning, I knew I would have to relinquish them.

In another encounter:

I then began having the sensation that people were attempting to get through to me, as if I were unconscious, and they were trying to establish communication and rouse me. I had the frightening thought that I might "come to" in someone else's body—in someone else's life—and would have no memory of my other life. It seemed very plausible, in that state, that such occurrences could take place.

On another occasion:

———

At one point I felt as if I were being drawn in by a man sitting on the ground. As if he were "dreaming" me and I could wake up as him. He seemed to be a man known affectionately in the village—perhaps an uncle of the boys. It seemed that he could be a sorcerer—calling me into appearing there.

———

In a subsequent encounter, I had the distinct impression that I was lying on the ground in a semisleeping state. A group of people stood hovering over me, evidently attempting to rouse me from my torpor. As I was beginning to awaken, I looked around to view my surroundings. I saw a group of black men or, more specifically, a group of legs standing around me. The legs were thin, with bare feet. The men seemed to be wearing long white shorts. The scene seemed to almost allude to an African or Haitian village. The reality of the scene was such that I felt as if I could have easily awoken into that world. Of course, in the calm light of day, such an occurrence seems an absurdity; but in a state of timeless, thoughtless perception, such reassurances are meaningless.

Other instances of contact were of a less frightening nature, being more of the nature of a friendly beckoning:

In the next moment, I felt the presence of someone to my left, over my shoulder specifically, whispering into my ear. The presence was an older male, not really a fatherly figure, but not devoid of feeling. He reminded me of an uncle I'd had growing up—not that I thought it "was" him, but the feelings generated were not dissimilar to that type of connection. He was reassuring, yet impartial. He seemed to be trying to instruct me in a technique for leaving the body. The technique consisted of his coaxing me to let go and drift toward him. The scene was reminiscent of an adult teaching a child to swim. I trusted him, although there was no feeling of what one might describe as benevolence on his part.

As this coaxing continued, I was also analyzing my somatic state. I felt virtually no physical sensations, as in normal waking awareness. I felt disconnected from all sensation, and therefore from any sensation of my body. It seemed that it was precisely because of this state that I could indeed drift and let go. I allowed myself to respond to his instructions and could feel myself letting go. At this point, I have no recollection of what transpired, although this might have simply been an exercise, for my benefit, in relinquishing somatic control. Suffice it to say that I reemerged slowly into my normal awareness, within a normal time frame.

The feeling that I was gradually being instructed was exhilarating. The mode of that instruction was not words or thoughts but a type of organic, somatic knowledge. I perceived a range of physical sensations that was intimately connected with my ordinary system of defining the world. As my perceptions became more precise and fluid, my dogmatic bias concerning the physical world was beginning to lose its prestige.

One aspect of the salviaic experience that was becoming clearer to me as time went on was that the depth of the state to which I'd become accustomed was only reached after passing a certain threshold of "intoxication." It was becoming apparent that there was a line of delineation below which, although under the effects of salvia, was, for me, ineffectual and ultimately without merit.

During this period, I experimented in the use of the tincture once again. Although the effects of the salvia were decidedly present, I was still primarily in my ordinary mode of awareness. I was aware of my surroundings and could have come out of the experience easily. My thought processes, although tinged with abstraction and captivated by light visions, were essentially unchanged. The gate hadn't been crossed. Without knowing it, I had inadvertently become accustomed to the blissful relinquishing of thought. Without that functional element of the trance, it seemed that nothing could be achieved. This point of delineation, strangely, was a very precise point.

One experience that occurred years later, while experimenting with a less potent batch of salvia, detailed this "crossing point":

———

Interesting experiment today. Since the "shrinking of the self"* was such a central theme the last time, I thought that perhaps, if I smoked a small amount of native leaf, this state could be accessed without the full-fledged shifting of awareness that happens with the 5X. The Wasson clone leaf had precisely that effect when I'd first sampled it years ago. At the time, I'd smoked one pipeful and experienced the shrinking of the self to a marked degree. I remember thinking then that, if nothing else, this leaf would be good for accessing that particular state. I might have smoked it once since then, but had thought it too weak for my normal excursions.

I loaded the bowl and smoked. The leaf seemed much harsher than either the Mazatecan or the Oaxacan leaf I'd used in the past. After exhaling, I got a few of the familiar signs of the salviaic trance—fluid kaleidoscopic manifestations—some fleeting emotionally tinged images of people—but nothing strong enough to "take" me. The

---

*I've endeavored to describe this unique state in detail in a subsequent chapter.

experience was short lived, and I thought that perhaps the leaf was even weaker than I'd recalled. I thought that it was more evident than ever that the leaf simply lacked enough strength to be usable. There was no shrinking of the self, for which I'd been hoping.

After a few minutes had passed, I thought that perhaps, if I smoked another bowl, the salvia might have a bit of a cumulative effect, since I could still feel the afterglow and thought that I might have more access to the shrinking awareness. I loaded the pipe again with a small amount, hoping that I could gently ease my way up with this second pipe.

After exhaling the smoke, I was amazed to find myself slipping, blissfully, to the other side. This happened so gently that it seemed as though I had time to analyze the process of the shift. From the first effects, it felt as though I was entering a deeper state than I'd anticipated. At some juncture, it seemed that I had encountered a point of no return. I began to feel myself sliding upward, as if I had no control, and unwittingly found myself in the other realm.

There were the others there, and I was almost in an apologetic frame of mind, as if to say, "Sorry, I didn't mean to cross over, it was an accident." I had the feeling that they, for their part, didn't care. It almost seemed as though they passed the word along to others as I went deeper into the other side. I also had the feeling that I was perfectly welcome there, at one point getting the feeling (not sure if someone said this) that it was good for me to just be in their presence, as if these contacts would have a cumulative effect: all in all, a very blissful, enjoyable, if accidental, meeting.

One small detail that I took note of this time occurred just as I was beginning to slide upward. It seemed as if some part of myself was gently shutting, almost the way one's eyes shut when falling asleep—although this seemed more pronounced and definite—akin to swallowing rather than a gradual closing of the eyes. It was almost as if a part of myself closed to the normal world so that I would be able to traverse the other. The aspect that struck me as interesting was that it was of the nature of a gate that was either open or shut to the world at large. After returning to normal awareness, it also gave the impression of being analogous to the valves in the heart that will shut to prevent blood from flowing backward. It appeared somehow significant that this gate seemed to have such a physical, organic structure. Although I didn't actually see it, but only felt or sensed it, again, like swallowing, it was evidently controlling the shifting or movement of awareness itself—almost as if it were preventing that awareness from flowing back into the ordinary world.

Although there was a very pronounced afterglow, there was still no shrinking of self. Perhaps this is determined by other factors and may not be as easily elicited as I'd hoped.

———

Such experiences almost seemed to add an air of precision to the process of transition and reinforced the seemingly organic substructure that defined such abstract psychological nuances.

3

AUGMENTATION

During the first two years of my salvia explorations, additional aspects of the experiences were becoming more and more apparent with the passage of time. What at first appeared to be peripheral occurrences, with time, deepened, and began to evince a more central role in the trance.

Perhaps the most significant of these aspects was the gradual realization that, at a certain point in the initial entering of the state, there occurred a unique transformation in the area of language. This was so subtle that only with repeated trials, as well as a deliberate focus on the actual mode of perceptual transformation, did it become apparent that it held, not a peripheral role, but a central one.

At a certain point after entering the state, the language that would normally describe, in an internal, almost unconscious way, the scenes, thoughts, and images that arrive through the senses would change. It would cease to be English. This apparent absurdity proved to be not only what might be perceived as an arbitrary adjunct to the experience, but an essential component of the change of awareness that entailed so many incomprehensible facets. It was as if the language itself was inexorably linked to the perceptual changes intrinsic to the state. It almost seemed as though the rapidity and depth of the experiences necessitated its own mode of communication.

Since the defining modality of these experiences was proving to be the cessation of thought, it follows that the normal process of language would also have to undergo a radical change. It goes without saying that normal language depends wholly on memory for every aspect of its functioning. If the memory itself ceases to function, as was becoming apparent in the salviaic state, language, as we know it, must also cease. It's as if the feather-light swiftness of the state can't bear the slow weight of words, or at least normal words.

The language that characterizes the trance state is, like so many other aspects of the salviaic state, at once totally foreign, yet somehow utterly familiar. After I began suspecting that there was indeed a change of language, I endeavored to observe the exact point of the shift, to observe the nuances of this change. What I found was that there occurred an all but unnoticeable transition into this new mode of communication. It was as if the vignettes that would present themselves would have a certain "flavor" of foreignness. As this foreign nature would become more obvious, it seemed there would come a point at which I would question, in some very primitive, immediate manner, whether the scene I was witnessing was disturbingly alien or secure and familiar.

At the same time, as these foreign occurrences would begin to manifest, this new language, as well, would begin to make its appearance. As I mentioned above, this alien language would begin to enter the context of the vignettes in an essentially seamless fashion. I would find myself witnessing a scene that was, in effect, being described in this new language. As a result of this change of conceptual matrix, the scene would then transform, in a most subtle fashion, into something comprehensible. The fact that I was so focused on this point of change also reinforced my observation that this language is a genuine auditory process—that it is actually "heard," in effect, with the ear, although, of course, this is an inner process.

I can think of no parallels in our ordinary experience, with the exception, perhaps of those circumstances where one hears one's name being called just after falling asleep. The latter can be an experience startling to the point of wakefulness. While the salviaic voices are merely part of the progressing vision, the distinct auditory nature is not dissimilar. The paradoxical nature of this new language was such that, although recognizable initially as foreign, it was also totally comprehensible. One would scarcely even notice the transition, since this other language is completely understandable and dovetails so appropriately with the new state in which one finds oneself. At this point, I'm not certain that I've spoken this language, although on a few rare occasions I have spoken a word or phrase. I can only surmise that it was through this medium, since normal words would be unbearably cumbersome and irretrievably out of reach.

On one occasion, after this language shift became more apparent, I attempted to "bring back a word." My notes, written the next day, can illustrate the experience:

————— ⊸ ⊸ —————

On this occasion, after entering, I was told by someone that I "had something there" (the word something, of course, was not actually used); what it was, was unclear. The meaning, though, was that I had some type of essentially "physical" connection to this other world. That connection consisted in this "something." At that point, I made the decision to attempt to remember or "take back" the word that described my connection with them. I, in effect, "held on" to this word, holding it to my chest. The form of this word was like a bowl—the open end being pressed to my chest, my arms wrapping around the bottom of the bowl. The sensation that ensued was not unlike traveling upward through water, clutching the treasure I'd retrieved from the depths. When I surfaced and began to reintegrate, I understood the word to be "name." I had succeeded in bringing back a word from the other world. Although the word, over there, was not in our language, the concept it represented seemed to translate to a concept in our language, namely the concept of "name."

I felt that the import of the experience was that I, in effect, had a "name" there and that this somehow insured my connection with that world. The concept of name was not concerned with appellation, but more with some primitive type of signature.

One of the features that seems to predominate in this language is a sense of "weighted" words or phrases. More often than not, a single phrase can contain, apart from the actual words themselves, a whole spectrum of affiliated meaning. It's as if the word or phrase is merely a vehicle for an entire constellation of images and meanings that is complex, yet completely understandable.

Aside from the flavor of foreignness, there is also the feeling of a nagging familiarity. I've found that this feeling of familiarity stems from the fact that this language, which is so distinct and alien, is very similar to, if not identical with, the language of dreams. Until my experimentation with salvia, I was never aware that such a dream language existed. I'm now convinced that it does, since so many of these salviaic episodes mimic the aura of deep dreams, only allowing one to maintain a focused and uninterrupted awareness that normally recedes during sleep. The similarity between the two is not as strange as might appear on the surface.

With the onset of sleep, the mind begins to relax, dream images first begin to make their appearance, and the descent into increasingly abstract mentation commences. Within a few moments, the burden of thought begins to lift, and one begins to lose consciousness. Thought has essentially stopped at this point. In deep dreamless sleep, there is no remembrance of the self—no memory, no words. There are no concepts to be upheld. There is no time. After what seems only moments, one becomes aware of the first inklings of awakening. The cumbersome chore of donning thought begins. The oppressive mental armor that had been shed now has to be lifted and put in place once again. One awakens.

In the midst of this seemingly timeless state, dreams can come. Of course, the majority of dreams are what might be characterized as "surface dreams" that replay events or concerns of the day. They can be almost annoying at times—repetitive, exhausting. They seem to occur just under the mantle of sleep and seem to be a mixture of sleep and waking. There can be other, deeper dreams as well. These are the dreams that seem richer and fuller.

These are the types that appear to parallel, in some ways, the salviaic state. Although these dreams are peopled with those we know, often those people shift, combine with, or are transformed into other people. Sometimes our companions are a mere voice or a presence, sometimes merely a feeling. Total strangers can make an appearance as well— sometimes with remarkably memorable features.

Intense emotions can also move us to laughter or tears in this state. These dreams can have their own form of language as well. How often have we found ourselves describing the content of a dream to someone in a fashion similar to the following: "He told me he was going on vacation, but somehow what this really meant was that he was going to the forest to live as a monk." This is the type of weighted phrase that occurs in the salviaic state. It seems that if one were in the depths of sleep, any transition to a new mode of language would have to go unnoticed.

This dream language that seems to be at the core of the salviaic state uses words that represent concepts in that mode of mentation. These concepts, it seems, can only be grasped in their entirety while in that state, but it seems that this dream language also partakes of a universal character, since many of the concepts represented are of a universal character. The references to the "land" or "place" of the dead, for instance, have by their nature a universal human resonance. The concepts of kinship and familial affection, for example, do not derive from concepts dependent on any one language.

The Swedish Christian mystic Emanuel Swedenborg spent much of his life exploring trance states that elucidated many concepts that find parallels in the salviaic state. His thoughts on language are particularly interesting in the present context:

> Hence it is that men while living in the body cannot speak with each other except by means of languages distinguished into articulate sounds, that is, into words, and are unable to understand one another unless they are acquainted with these languages, for the reason that their speech is from the exterior memory. Whereas spirits speak with each other by means of a universal language distinguished into ideas such as are of thought itself, and thus they can have converse with any spirit whatever, of whatever language and nation he had been while in the world, for the reason that their speech is from the interior memory. Into this language comes every man immediately after death, because he comes into this memory, which, as before said, is proper to his spirit.*

---

*Emanuel Swedenborg, *Arcana Coelestia* vol. 3, revised and edited by John Faulkner Potts (West Chester: Swedenborg Foundation, 1984). Reprinted by permission of the Swedenborg Foundation.

In addition to the perceptual changes involving language, there were also perceptual factors involving somatic processes. To characterize these factors as purely physiological would be inaccurate. These perceptions would also entail vivid psychological and emotional components.

One such factor, which I began to experience about a year into my involvement with salvia and which continues to this day, I initially referred to in my notes as a "breakthrough into purity." My entry following one such experience can illustrate:

One perception that has been repeatedly experienced has been an emotional feeling coupled with a somatic sensation, seemingly centered in the head of what one might describe as "purity."

It seems to result from the sensation of "pushing up through layers." On one level this feels as if it's occurring physically within the brain on some sort of neural level—it could be described as a blissful, even ecstatic combination of centering and relaxation on one hand, with an attitude of focused endeavor on the other. At the same time, one feels as if one is pushing up or through some sort of barrier or doorway into another realm.

The aftereffect of this combination of somatic and psychological experiences is a sensation—also somatic as well as psychological—of a type of blissful neural "freshness" that seems centered somewhere behind the eyes. The feeling seems at once natural, primitive, and restorative.

———

This experience of freshness or purity is unique, in my experience, to salvia. The feeling is not unlike a type of birth—as if one had just emerged from a cocoon of some sort. There is a sense of exhilarating newness, as if one were a new bud pushing out from a branch. The accompanying somatic component is correspondingly rapturous. There seems to be an inherent blissful nature to reproductive processes, and this process seems to echo that function. The sensation has a cerebral focus, almost akin to a sort of ecstatic "itching" behind the eyes and up through the crown of the head. Since this experience is not a direct facet of the salviaic trance per se, but is a manifestation of the afterglow state, there is time to analyze these sensations in some depth. I've found that this perception of purity can last about ten minutes after reintegration.

Another, more subtle aspect of this blissful sensation that I've come to notice, with time, is that it always seems, on some level, to be intrinsically tied to the concept of death. It's as if this purity is the "other side" of death—a natural unity that we can inherently sense on some primitive level. At times these sensations can seem like vague memories, on a level that defies description. The continued references to the "place of the dead," as well as the corresponding perceptual occurrences, serve to reinforce this connection. Salvia alone, it seems, can afford one access to this paradoxical perception of "blissful death flesh."

During this same period of time, yet another strange series of vignettes would present themselves. During the course of my salvia excursion, there would come a point, which I later surmised to be a type of cresting of the experience, which was, in effect, the culmination of awareness and sensory transformation. As the intensity of the experience was just beginning to recede, a disquieting event would occur. I would, without warning, begin to see what could only be described as animate corpses. The first time this occurred, I was afraid that I was being delivered over to an alternate group of presences, who had a darker side than those to which I'd become accustomed. It seemed that, all at once, what had been a transcendent, exhilarating experience had been transformed into a dark, foreboding, sorrowful realm. The beings that heralded this change were gaunt, exaggerated, skeletal forms, with long, bony, almost insectlike arms. They bore ancient parched faces and seemed to personify decrepit frailty. This, needless to say, was somewhat frightening, although, since the tenor of the salviaic visions was generally of such a bizarre nature, it seemed unnecessary to overreact. Although, after first noticing these vignettes followed the ingestion of a certain type of 5X, I must admit that I avoided that particular preparation for a while.

With time, these presences lost their foreboding nature. Like so many other facets of the salviaic trance, what initially could seem horrific, with time, would lessen in magnitude and become accepted as an intrinsic component of the event. Fear would be replaced with a consuming curiosity. It subsequently became commonplace to see the corpses as my journey was nearing its completion. It was as if my skeletal companions were announcing that I would be leaving the swift fluid darkness and returning to the anguished world of flesh and time.

These images persisted for several months as a regular component of my journeys, and although they've subsequently made an appearance on occasion, they've generally discontinued.

4
TAKEN

As time went on, I became increasingly familiar with the salviaic trance in general, as well as with its multilayered perceptual nuances. Yet one aspect was a bit unnerving. It could be characterized as a state-specific phenomenon,* although the strangeness of the experience seemed to imply much more.

As I've mentioned, it was a regular feature of my excursions to encounter very ordinary appearing "people." These people would be the players in varied vignettes and, on occasion, would interact directly with me through speech, action, and so forth. Although this was quite a startling

---

*This phenomenon is one that is usually associated with hallucinogenic use, wherein a series of thoughts, perceptions, and the like are forgotten after returning to one's ordinary awareness, yet come into memory once again the next time one enters the hallucinogenic state.

development, it always felt as if there was some type of distance between us. The vignettes were almost dreamlike at times, although the vividness as well as the continuity of awareness radically differentiated the two states.

What began to happen, over a period of months, was that the tenor of my encounters began to achieve an immediacy—a reality that was genuinely startling. I would relive this almost comical scenario every time I would smoke. I would try to prepare myself mentally, aware that I would soon be in the presence of the "others"; this, of course, was easy enough in the safety of my ordinary world. This was nothing new—I was used to this. Then I would smoke. All of a sudden the reality of the other world and its inhabitants would wash over me like an icy wave. It would become disturbingly apparent that this realm of experience is the real one. This world is the real world—not the contrived world of personality, ideas, and thoughts that insulates us from the infinite—that coddles us into clinging desperately to the known. What was beginning to happen was an almost syntactical transformation of the others from the third person to the second person.

Shortly after smoking, as the foundation of my world was beginning to crumble, I would be "taken." There's almost no other way to characterize it—I felt as if I were being literally whisked away to something indescribable. My guides were also becoming more present than ever before. These events were becoming more and more intensely personal, on a level that, several months before, I, myself, would have equated with madness. I found that, although I knew what to expect, there was really no way to prepare myself for these encounters. The alien nature of this realm precluded this, as well as the fact that I, myself, would, in effect, change during these events. The part of myself that attempted to prepare would evaporate as thought and memory would cease. The intense reality of these engagements would consistently take me by surprise.

To our normal way of thinking, to be "taken" would imply some sense of physical displacement, but in this case it seems that one is taken more to a state of being—or, more precisely, to a state of contact. At times, the visions that would present themselves would be of a more vague nature, yet the palpable sense of being taken would be undeniably intense. It seemed as though this sense of contact was, in itself, the transformative element. It's as if by the lightest touching of this state, one was somehow changed. It seemed as though this contact, by its very nature, was the mechanism for the resultant blissful awareness.

On many occasions, I would want to lightly access the state as a way of exploring the nature of the transition, or merely to have a less intense experience. I would smoke one bowl of Oaxacan leaf in these cases. Even then, profound experiences could result.

From my notes, written immediately after returning:

———

One bowl Oaxacan:

Went all the way in and was totally absorbed by the other world and its inhabitants.

Sitting here now, I'm still amazed at the totality of my departure on one bowl. I felt completely disconnected with this world—totally immersed. I was very comfortable and felt very much at home there, relatively, anyway. There was a group of young men engendering feelings of some sort of familial brotherhood. One of the brothers jokingly asked something to the effect of, "What am I supposed to do with him (meaning me, since I wasn't dead)?" This was a rhetorical question, and there seemed to be a good-natured feel to this. There were other people around, as well, but they were more of the nature of peripheral presences.

I had the definite feeling that this realm is above and beyond death—a feeling that the awareness that's characterized by this state doesn't die. Not unlike a Swedenborgian "state."*

I also felt, in the initial phase, that the cartoon characters (of my first experiences) are the people there, talking to us on some level of primitive emotional communication. That mode of communication is just

———

*Swedenborg described heaven and eternity as being essentially outside of time, being a perception of degree or "state."

unknown to us—a foreign emotional language.

There seemed to be quite a bit of talking this time. Again, the language appears to be some sort of "native tongue" but alien to our ordinary state. On more than one occasion, I've gotten the impression that the language there is experientially more rapid than ours. It seems, also, to be a more "interior" (again, a Swedenborgian term) language.

———————

At this time, I also began experimenting with multiple back-to-back excursions, smoking perhaps three or four times in one afternoon, with about thirty minutes between sessions. I would generally use one bowl of the weaker Oaxacan leaf at each session. On one such trial, I had the opportunity to smoke in a small isolated cabin in the woods near my home. I had begun to smoke during the afternoon, rather than later at night. I felt that salvia could be enough of a disorienting experience and that to reemerge into a familiar secure environment was decidedly more reassuring than finding oneself in total darkness.

Looking out on the forest on a warm summer day could be very comforting. On one such trial, I had smoked the milder leaf twice, but felt nothing significant. I had had mild, almost annoying visions both times. The scenarios seemed weak and arbitrary. My frame of mind was not good. I thought that perhaps I was wasting my time. I was

tired of these vignettes to nowhere. This very leaf had cata-
pulted me deeply into the other world on a regular basis,
now I was spinning my wheels. I thought I'd give it one
more try, just to be sure. I lit the pipe again and smoked
with an unusual vehemence.

What happened next was almost indescribable. I was,
it seemed, literally dragged out of my body so forcefully
and so completely that I was sure I had died. I plummeted
upward so rapidly that any thought, or even sustained perception, was out of the question. I was dying, no doubt.
The experience of dying was not a thought but more a
sense that everything I knew was being wrenched from my
hands. Again, although this event was frightening in one
sense, it also gave the distinct impression that this was a
totally natural circumstance. In an inexplicable way, it felt
right. It also felt oddly familiar, as if this occurrence was
not outside the sphere of experiences that make up the
totality of humanness. I mean to infer nothing here, but to
fail to note these perceptual impressions would render an
incomplete, if not inaccurate, assessment of my experience.

During this occurrence, since thought was essentially
absent, fear, also, was unable to get a foothold in the usual
manner. Everything was happening too rapidly. Awe, rather
than anguish, prevailed. After the session had come to a
close, I was more convinced than ever that salvia had some
genuine affinity with the process of death—not in any mor-
bid aspect, but in an almost comforting, revelatory manner.

It seemed that one could explore the process of death this way.

I continued with my pursuit of multiple trials using weaker salvia. This method, although occasionally frustrating, could also evince a cumulative effect at times. On one such occasion I smoked salvia several times over the course of a few hours. Aside from the opportunity to observe some of the peculiarities, as well as the quantitative abundance of the language spoken during one session, the first few trials were uneventful and disappointing. At this point, I again felt frustrated with my lack of results.

On my last attempt, I was determined to break through and loaded the pipe with the stronger Mazatecan leaf. I felt almost demanding and inhaled deeply. To my relief, this time was different—I had broken through to the state I'd wanted. I strongly felt the familiar physical sensations—the familiar shift. I suddenly found myself staring at a "nest" of organisms. Their shape was rounded, undefined—soft and egglike. There were dozens, perhaps hundreds, of them immersed in some type of thick fluid matrix. At the same time, I heard a voice say something to this effect, "It's all right, you only wanted to be among your own kind." This was evidently an explanation for my mood of vehemence in smoking this last time. I indeed felt that I was among my own "kind" in the nest. It sounds implausible, yet there was an overwhelming feeling of affection for these organisms. It was as though affection and kinship is not the sole domain of humankind. Again, this feeling of kinship entailed what might be characterized as familial or tribal overtones.

In the moments that followed, I became very strongly aware of a blissful pins-and-needles feeling that was, although naturally tactile in nature, somehow outside the sphere of my ordinary physical body. The perceptions were mental, yet had some mode of physicality as their base. The same voice spoke again saying something to the effect of, "All right, this is the flesh of the gods."*

My perception was of a secondary or mental body that was "over there." The sensations of my normal physical body had ceased—I was beginning to perceive sensations from this other "body," this other "flesh." These sensations were what appeared to be normal tactile impressions, in one sense; yet, at the same time, they possessed what might be termed a blissful fluidity that could herald immeasurable perceptual possibilities. This perception of the secondary body was, although necessarily fleeting, distinct and palpable. I also had the distinct impression that this series of perceptions was given to me as a gift.

---

*I had been aware of the phrase "flesh of the gods" in reference to hallucinogenic mushrooms. I was under the impression that this was an ancient term, going back before the conquest, used to describe the mushrooms themselves. This was a new context for the phrase that was unfamiliar, since it described a distinct somatic perception, rather than the mushrooms that might engender such a perception.

It occurred to me that, to have this type of perception, I must have died, but somehow I knew (perhaps I was reassured, in some way) that I hadn't. Shortly after this, I came to normalcy, but the "flesh of the gods" experience was unique—not only due to the experience itself, but also because of how it was demonstrated to me in such a remarkable yet understandable manner.

It became obvious that what we perceive as physicality is not really a direct tactile perception from our body but a translation of sensations by some aspect of the psyche, which interprets and describes the body's signals. It's as if we feel a certain constellation of sensations, and our mind translates this as "hand" or "left leg," but in the end, it is the mind that is describing and hence creating the body. In this particular experience, my mind was perceiving a group of sensations and was describing it again, as "hand," and so on, but the sensations this time originated from a source other than the normal physical matrix. These alternate sensations were still translated, however, as a "body."

This was perhaps the most dramatic revelation of a secondary body I'd encountered. The perception of this alternate physical body has been a recurring motif in many of my sessions with salvia. Many times I've felt as if I were gradually developing, or learning the mode of perceiving, this alternate body. Strange as it would seem from an ordinary standpoint, it seems almost logical, since the normal physical body is, at this point, essentially inoperable—that to perceive and possibly to act in this alternate realm, one would need a corresponding vehicle for perception.

On another occasion, this emphasis on the new body was also predominant. From my notes, written immediately afterward:

Immediately "taken," I began to emerge into some type of hall, not unlike a wedding reception. An older man was guiding me saying, "Come on . . . Come on . . ." as if he were somehow guiding or coaching me. People were present observing as if watching a birth. I was given to understand that I was being "born" there. I was almost "out"—people were happily anticipating my birth. The thought crossed my mind that perhaps I was dying, but didn't feel that that was the case.

It seems as though perhaps this is what's occurring— I'm slowly being born over there, and almost made it through this time. I'm afraid that I was still a bit hesitant to burst through completely, since there's always anxiety about returning. The place and the people are less alien now, and their presence is always anticipated with something approaching longing. At one point while I was being born, I asked something about language to the effect of, "How can I be here and not know the language?" No one answered me, but I felt that they knew it wouldn't be a problem.

Again, this time I felt I was going in very deeply and only hanging by a thread here. I also felt that I had total trust in my new situation.

———

The recurring themes of language and tactile perceptions could occasionally take remarkable turns. In one such session, the possibilities of perceptual transformation seemed to know no limits. It seemed that humanness itself was, in the end, essentially also a habitual interpretation.

Again, my notes immediately following the event might convey better the sense of immediacy, with more accuracy:

———

Made some sort of breakthrough tonight—very strong effect. They were aware that I was "making a bridge" to their world. They had some sort of word or phrase for what I was doing, which connoted somehow trying to explain something here, or maintain some sense of lucidity. Very many "thought states." Would have been afraid I'd forget how to get back—could not have found my old body and mind on my own—matter of some sort of faith.

I might have been analyzing the language to some extent. I was led upward, apparently by a woman, into an "upper room" or state of language. She was showing me the secret of their language, which entailed physiological or somatic-tactile elements, rather than verbal formulations. I found myself emerging into some sort of viscous cocoon or hivelike structure, peopled by insects or some sort of insect-type beings, of which I was one. We were not unlike mantises or grasshoppers. We had some type of long thin insect legs, which we were pressing against the surrounding viscous substance that seemed sticky or stringy. This was how they were able to communicate—on an insect level. I was being shown this as a privilege. I understood completely how this could be the essence of their language and their mode of communication. The other insect beings I sensed, somehow, to be female and young. The woman (she was almost like the "den mother" of the young insects in the cocoon) who escorted me there was not particularly friendly—my recollection is that she had a human form, but this is very vague. It seemed more of an annoyance that she had to show me this scene. I didn't sense any malevolence on her part, however.

The insect forms cleared up some strange images I'd encountered before: batlike beings crawling on bony wings and sticklike people that I would encounter toward the end of a session. This made all those images clear, as if they were a prefigurement of that mode of communication.

This particular mode of communication, as well as the physical form of my own body and those of my companions, has not been repeated, although I'm sure that this area of perception will, in the future, be revisited. To speculate on various aspects of this incident, which was among the strangest of my encounters, would be pointless. The foreign nature of these events seems to demand experiential, rather than discursive, exploration.

Many more excursions tended to be somehow connected with the process or concept of death and an apparent realm of the dead. The focus of a great number of experiences was an exploration of some aspect of this journey. Often there would be others present, perhaps in a peripheral context, who, I was given to understand, were the newly dead. As strange or improbable as this might sound, it was repeated so often, and in so many ways, that I was constrained to regard this as an emotional certainty during the course of the trance.

One such occasion was very explicit and succinct:

——— ———

Smoked one bowl 5X, E. present:

I felt very secure going in, with no fear. Went through the usual multiple realms, finally surfacing. It was as if I were some type of organic protuberance on a membrane. The membrane seemed fleshy, like the inside of the mouth. "They" came to me as if they were needed in some way.

They seemed to approach me by somehow sensing my sudden appearance, not unlike bees sensing a flower and approaching (this was the image that was offered). They led me to understand that they had some sort of function with the dead, as if they were escorting them. It was as though they were on the lookout for the newly dead (as from drowning and so forth) and would, on some organic level, sense them through scent. They would flock to them and apparently escort them, possibly, for the purpose of continuing a chain of human contact. It seemed as if I was seen as a false alarm.

It once again seemed like a very normal process connected with death. The continuity of these states only seems to reinforce the certainty of the reality and the normalcy of this process. Where the newly dead are escorted is still unknown.

In another trial, a British family made their appearance. I thought at first that perhaps they were sent to guide me, but had the distinct feeling that they were among the newly dead. The father (I didn't actually see the family, but knew there was a mother and two children—a son and a daughter) seemed pleasant but somewhat confused and disoriented. This scene seemed particularly sad, due, no doubt, to the implication that the family had perished together.

Another impression that was repeatedly given me was

that there were others in addition to myself who would also make their appearance here. On a few occasions, I was referred to as "one of them." From my notes:

Nice strong effect. It seemed as though I went through some sort of membrane, not unlike coming into a clearing after wading through tall grass.

I was immediately met by presences, two young boys who could have been twins, about ten or eleven years old with short, black hair. They began to announce to someone (their mother?) that "One of them was here," as if someone had just appeared in their midst. This seemed as if it were not a particularly rare occurrence. I had the distinct impression (from their voice—perhaps an accent?) that they were Mexican.

When they announced my presence, they described me as one of "them," implying "those who are willing to die to be here." At the time, I understood it to mean that dying (through hallucinogenic states) was a way of entering their world. It also implied that normal death would be the usual mode for such an entry.

This particular event serves as a good example of the type of communication that is prevalent in this state. Although there were only a few words spoken, each of these words, or perhaps more precisely the content engendered by the phrase, contained a wealth of images and meanings that were as profound as they were comprehensible.

Again, the mode of this type of communication seems similar, if not identical, to that which is so recognizable in dreams. This recurrence of words and phrases, so laden with emotional and psychological meaning, combined with the ravenous awareness engendered by salvia, leads to a singularly rich assimilation of conceptual images that is both distinct and instantaneous.

This perception that I was not alone in visiting this realm was reinforced several times. From my notes:

One bowl Oaxacan:

Had been awhile since I'd smoked. I was able to analyze early perceptions. There seemed to be nodes in my visual field in a symmetrical pattern, with maybe five or six points of focus. The visual field flowed, opened from them, and wrapped around them, as if they were centers of gravity. The field encircled the whole configuration, and I was "there."

As usual, there were people there acknowledging my arrival. There seemed to be some sort of noting that I was different from them—not in a pejorative sense, but mentioned in passing, as if to say, "Here's a guy from there, or here's a guy that comes that way." Some sign was made—putting hands toward the face or fingers to lips, in some fashion, to signify this. Nothing important in this, just noted it.

———

On another occasion, I was given the impression that there is a mutual link between both worlds that seemed to hint at some form of interdependence:

———

One bowl:

Young boy, perhaps eight or nine, and his little sister answered the door. The boy said something to the effect of, "They needed one, anyway," meaning his family needed a witness, or contact, or recorder from this world, as if they also need contact here and need someone as a conduit. The feeling, maybe third time I'm getting this, is that I am also useful somehow to them.

———

There are a certain number of perceptions, such as those mentioned above, that make their appearance so often during the course of repeated sessions as to give the impression that they are intrinsic to the state. During many trials, after first entering the trance, I've witnessed a succession of innumerable scenarios detailing various events and vignettes with an eerily comforting demeanor. These visions portray remarkably ordinary occurrences that have a profound, yet disturbing, sense of familiarity. Scenes of people engaged in commonplace pursuits seem to predominate. This process seems to occur shortly after entering the deeper trance state.

There inevitably comes a point, upon entering the rush of visions, that one can't decide if the scenes being witnessed are those that would occur in the normal range of events, with which we are familiar, or if these are actually quite alien occurrences, suddenly comprehensible due to the exhaustive alteration of awareness. Ironically, there is no benchmark against which one can compare these scenes. There is no longer any valid measure of experience. It seems impossible to retrieve one of these visions and bring it back for examination. The seemingly ordinary nature of these scenes is by no means a guarantee of their genesis from our world. The impression, in fact, is that the opposite is true; these scenarios, while exhibiting the trappings of routine, are, in fact, essentially alien.

One element that had made its appearance in a few of the previous experiences was the impression that my "hosts" were directly endeavoring to teach me or perhaps more precisely indicate those circumstances in which I might learn:

Upon entering, I felt very focused yet without thought. A voice implied that this transcendence was possible because

I'd relinquished my mind, which could then be manipulated. I felt that I was totally abandoned as far as my mind went and was entirely thoughtless. I could feel how my mind was almost sectioned or diced by a kaleidoscopic dimension. There were images of people or, rather, interactions with people. An older woman began explaining that she would be responsible for my mind, or, more precisely, she would be willing to avail her services of manipulating my mind and thus my perceptions. There was no emotional content to this—it seemed more of a contractual nature. She was in a way offering her services.

On another occasion that took place about a year later, I found myself in a more direct teaching situation:

I found myself in the presence of a person who was evidently a "teacher" of sorts, but more in the nature of a "coach." This person (black female, I believe, but not sure) was explaining that I was not alone, that there were others who also feared death and that that was normal— everyone fears death. While she was speaking, I felt that I was standing, perhaps sitting, shoulder to shoulder with other males. The impression was that they were, in effect, shamans-in-training and that we all were more or less at the same impasse, which is fear of death. The gist of the talk was that we were not alone and there was no problem—that we should feel ready, but at the same time no one is ever really ready. There seemed to be no need to hurry—merely to understand that it was a natural reaction and that we were not alone.

It felt as though this was training for learning to stay longer in the trance state.

The entire excursion was very reassuring in tone, yet somehow very exciting, since it seemed to be such a measured natural response. It was also very encouraging to be shoulder to shoulder with other pursuers.

If, indeed, there is some sort of contact between the two worlds, aside from the frequent references to the dead, it is in a form that is all but incomprehensible. My personal experience with the salviaic trance would have led me to the conclusion that the two states of awareness are, by their very nature, irreconcilable. Our normal framework for perception relies, it would seem, wholeheartedly on the foundation of thought. It defines our entire life, our perception of our physical body, and our environment; it, in effect, creates and sustains the solidity of our world.

The salviaic state, on the other hand, appears to consist of a mode of thoughtless awareness—a fluid, immediate, direct perception of forces and realms of interaction that have no reference from our normal standpoint. Even the habitual mode of perceiving from what one might refer to as a human vantage point is no longer sacrosanct.

Paradoxically, however, there does seem to be some type of communication between these two, apparently diametrically opposite modalities. Although in the deepest states of the trance, the overwhelming immersion in the state seems to admit no compromise, yet there do seem to be occasions of admixture between the two states during the course of the varying stages of the trance.

During my succeeding salvia sessions, something quite unusual began to occur. On several occasions I was given seemingly direct indications for behavior in the ordinary world. These indications were specifically concerned with my manner of approaching salvia. Up until this time, with rare exceptions, I had smoked salvia alone, in a small workshop near my house. I was well aware that many caution against such behavior, since people, under salvia's influence, have been known to move around, possibly injuring themselves. They generally advise using a "sitter" to be present during the salvia excursion, to protect and reassure the participant in the event of any untoward circumstances.

In my personal situation, I'd always felt that it was unnecessary. I never felt the need to move from my chair and felt that another person would be a distraction, inhibiting my spontaneous approach to smoking. I regarded salvia as a solitary pursuit. My "advisors," however, began to indicate that I should indeed have someone present, not for my physical safety, as such, but as a way of guarding my body. The implication was that at some point I would have to leave my body. I felt that this would entail losing consciousness, and someone should be there to aid in bringing me back, if needed.

———

After smoking about ten minutes previously:

My second excursion was incredible. I was already feeling a strong afterglow from the first experience, when I began the second round of smoking. Everything seemed already accessible, and I knew exactly where to go and what to do. It was almost as if I rode the afterglow behind my eyes, back to its source. It seemed to expedite and clarify the experience. I went in very deeply and strongly and was able to surrender myself to a very great degree. I seemed to be floating in a black or starry sky. The feeling of the presences was paramount.

There was an older woman, not unlike other personages I've encountered before. She seemed very similar to the woman who once told me I was accepted. She was doing something to my floating body, and seemed to be wrapping it, again, not unlike a cocoon, but using some sheetlike material. She told me in a matter-of-fact tone that if she was going to teach me she would need more time, and that I would have to stay longer, period.

This had some implication of language, as if she would instruct me through teaching me their language. The sense I got from her statement was that I was on the verge of letting go to an even greater extent and that this might allow them to take me for a longer period. The implication was that I should make arrangements, over here, for that occurrence. It was as if she were advising me to have someone here watching my body, in effect, so that I'd feel free to stay for an extended period. Without this extended stay, nothing would be possible.

As I emerged from the salvia, I felt as though I'd had a profound connection and invitation. I also saw, for the first time, how this might be possible. Perhaps the salvia and attendant presences could usher one into a trance that would extend beyond the duration of the salviaic trance. If this were the case, anything would be possible.

Although it seemed as though I should have someone present during my sessions, I felt that it might inhibit me on some level. I thought that I could still investigate the salviaic state to a great extent, as I had been. I felt that I had to mentally prepare myself before these excursions and that someone else's presence would negate the solitary nature of my preparation. It also seemed that it might just be an anomaly to have such an indication, that if I continued alone everything would still be safe; after all, even if I were to lose consciousness for a few moments, it wouldn't necessarily be life threatening.

In the months that followed, I continued my solitary pursuit of salvia, without incident. Many of the more interesting sessions, some details of which I've related above, occurred during this period.

During this time, many of my experiences began to exhibit details, on a surprisingly consistent basis, that had been hinted at, or perhaps alluded to, in past sessions. After smoking, I was increasingly finding myself in what might be characterized as a "Caribbean" environment. This place has no specific features that might readily identify it. The inhabitants are primarily black, although there seems to be an Indian presence. Often, there is a carnivallike atmosphere with people dancing in parades. The women wear bright-colored dresses with billowing skirts and some sort of headscarves. There is a feeling of a primitive naturalness, but with overtones of a hard life. At the same time, I continued to have the impression that I was somehow being cared for:

———

I went with them and was very clearly under the care of a younger, husky black woman. She was apparently from some Caribbean country. She seemed to be talking in a relaxed way with another woman. She didn't pay me any direct attention, but I was definitely in her charge. Almost as if I were a child she was "herding." It could have also been that she was in charge of leading me somewhere. This was her job. There was no personal contact between us, although I felt that I was clinging to her on some level, even if only figuratively—but there seemed to be more of a physical connection.

During this time, another remarkable experience reinforced the admonition to have someone present to guard my body. This particular incident was unique in that it represented a benchmark in my approach to salvia, since there occurred not only an astonishing quality of personal contact with someone who I felt I had definitely encountered before, but because the presence of this person exuded such a palpable aura of what can only be described as "power." From my notes:

One bowl 5X:

I was immediately taken. As I was entering, I noted the state of my mind, which had taken the same formless quality as yesterday. I believe it was at this juncture that I began to hear speech. I abandoned myself to the speaking and noticed that it was indeed a foreign tongue. It was not English or Spanish or anything familiar.

Shortly thereafter, there appeared a woman coming

*from my left moving toward the right. She began saying,
"Hope you've got one . . . hope you've got one!" This
meant someone to watch my body and keep me in this life.
I was aware that I didn't "have one" since I was alone. I'm
not sure of the language that she spoke. I seemed to hear
her in English, but it may have been the dream language
being spoken.*

*I felt that I was fluid and easily manipulated. Within
moments, a large black woman—seemingly Jamaican or
East Indian—appeared. Evidently, the first woman was
her assistant or perhaps part of her retinue. At any rate,
the black woman was the master of the show. She more
or less moved me on a whim. She was obviously in control
and was very powerful. I felt that she was what could only
be characterized as a "witch," though not necessarily evil,
just powerful. I realized I'd seen her before, but always in
a peripheral context, never realizing she was calling the
shots. The experience was intensely real and personal. I
felt as if many of my other journeys had been leading me
to this. It was as though my encounter with her was some
sort of turning point.*

*She seemed to have the power to take me away at will.
Even at this juncture, the events beheld still have a feeling
rooted in natural humanness. On some level, this is all a
natural unfolding of events. She is just skilled in something
we're totally unaware of, yet subject to.*

During her entrance, it seemed as if I were being

enveloped by an overwhelming rhythmical presence. I can't be certain if it was the drumming or the language, or perhaps a combination of both. In any event, the effect was to fascinate the attention and paralyze it. This enabled her to be in control. I felt she could have swept me away in an instant, had that been her wish.

The impressions left by this experience were profound. Encountering someone whom I'd met before was exhilarating in itself, since it revealed an internal consistency to the events I'd been witnessing. There was now a demonstrable unity to the locale and personages I'd encountered. For the first time, I actually felt that I had, in effect, a "contact," or perhaps a comrade in this alien realm. In addition, the demonstration of her power was remarkable. It seemed as though, through the rhythmical entrapment of the drumming, I felt like a fish on a hook. I was powerless to pull free. At the same time, my instructress was in complete control of my fate. Her power seemed to rest in the fact that she completely understood the mechanics of such enchantment and could utilize it as she wished. There was no pettiness, however; the fascination was in the wake of her "solidity."

Once again, these impressions, though seemingly bizarre, had an inherent core of naturalness that proved so prevalent in many of these experiences. The mechanism of power and fascination seemed to come from what might be characterized as a tribal knowledge—as if this interplay of forces is an integral part of physical interaction within a genuinely natural environment, from which we are so separate. It's as if this were an application of "higher physics" that could only be ascertained or perceived by a naturally functioning organism, whose perceptions were heightened to their natural state of animal sensitivity.

On another occasion, I was given what might be considered a very blunt indication that my mode of solitary investigation was misguided and should be amended. After smoking, I had my now familiar experience of relinquishing language. Words and phrases like "sitting in the shop" or "just smoked salvia" began to rapidly lose any meaning and were forcefully swept away by the wave of foreign images and feelings. The appearance of my guides, this time, was accompanied by a decided feeling of admonition. I found myself in the dark, looking toward the lights of a house. At the same time I was being told, in some manner, that this was a familial or tribal pursuit and that one does not follow it in a solitary fashion. It was implied that it was somehow for the benefit of a group that this contact was intended. Although there was a tone of rebuke to the experience, there was also a genuine feeling of instruction on an emotional level.

These admonitions were, I must admit, unwelcome, since it seemed that this type of exploration was an inherently solitary pursuit. If one must face suffering and death alone, it would seem that one would also encounter knowledge alone. To be connected, in a genuine way, to a tribal group would be a condition devoutly to be wished, in our cerebral, fragmented culture. It would tend to represent a culmination, rather than a starting point. Nevertheless, these admonitions of tribal representation continued in subsequent endeavors with salvia.

In another trial, about a month later, I was again encouraged to have a sitter present, but more for my own protection and instruction, rather than from any sense of duty to a communal or familial group.

From my notes:

———

After entering the state, I was taken in one of the most forceful manners yet. The force of transition was not unlike a magnetic or gravitational attraction that was all but irresistible. My initial perception was of some sort of surrounding rhythmical process, not unlike drumming or rattling. It was also akin to some sort of organic process such as the beating of the heart, only more rapid. This mesmerizing rhythmical pattern surrounded me and seemed to totally fascinate my attention. At the same time, the pulsing of the sound opened an awareness of a physical body in that realm. This sensation has happened before, wherein the normal physical body loses awareness and a new body, over there, gains awareness. This is not a very comfortable situation—in fact, it's quite frightening. The dream body doesn't seem to have any contact with anything solid, but one feels as though one is treading water in a black ocean. The only link with the "old" body seems to be in the breath.

This sensation, although frightening, was bearable, it seems, due to the degree of awareness that one enjoys in this state. One feels totally awake during this process and, on some level, maintains some feeling of will or intention. While this physical process of "sensing the dream body" was unfolding, there was also the appearance of my hosts in this realm.

The remarkable feature of this particular encounter was the direct conversational nature of the event. I use the word conversational in a limited way, since I said nothing but was being instructed by a younger black woman, who spoke to me in a very nonthreatening, personal manner about my situation.

She told me, in effect, that I should not leave my physical body alone like that, implying that it was somehow dangerous. She also told me, in a very direct way, that if I chose, I would be taken in the dream body with them and instructed. She was not alone, but I have no recollection of her companions. There appeared to be perhaps two other people. It seemed a prerequisite to be in this dream body in order to learn.

This learning, it seems, consisted of "absorbing gifts"

in the sense of physical units of knowledge. This knowledge was in the realm of awareness of one's perception of one's self and the world that one perceived. The awareness of the dream body would be one such unit of knowledge.

My instructress, again, seemed to be connected with some sort of organic tribal tradition. At one point, I had the distinct impression that she was African. Whether she told me this or not is unclear, although I have a lingering remembrance that she did.

This Afro-Caribbean context, although incomprehensible and very confusing in my ordinary world, has become quite familiar and almost reassuring in my salviaic encounters.

One salient feature of this particular excursion was the force of the attraction to join my hosts. It was only the admonition about leaving my body alone in that state that gave me pause to join them.

The idea that this type of endeavor has some function in a tribal grouping was reinforced in subsequent trials and began to serve almost as a subtext to many experiences.

On one such occasion, I was given to understand that I was in the care of, or associated with, a person (male) whose task was to somehow bring me to death. This was not a frightening event in any sense but, on the contrary, was magnificently joyous. There was an emotion akin to an exuberant excitement, coupled with what can only be described as a regal magnificence. There was an accompanying aesthetic rapture not dissimilar to being swept away by exquisite music. This taste of death was short lived but dramatic in its revelation of this strange union of death and joy.

After smoking a second time, shortly afterward, I found myself in the presence of "welcomers," an elderly man and his wife. There was a lighthearted tone to this meeting, the man joking with his wife that there was no need to get "dressed up," or something to that effect, since "he's not dead" meaning that I was a false alarm. I also found this very funny; the humorous tone lasted even after I returned to normalcy.

The gist of my instruction here, although not framed by any specific events, was a very obvious realization that, as humans, we need connections with the dead. Evidently, this is ideally accomplished by one member of each group, be it familial, tribal, or some other connection. It was implied that every small group of people should have one among them to remind them of the reality of death and to connect them to each other through this understanding. It seemed as though this is the natural order—to have a human connection with the other world.

The next day, I decided to smoke again. I immediately found myself emerging through the floor, it seemed, into a room with four or five men. They appeared to be Mexican or perhaps South American and were all wearing blue shirts that seemed to be part of a uniform. They were apparently workers, perhaps in a factory or plant of some sort. They gave the impression of being rugged or gruff somehow and seemed to have had hard lives.

As I arrived, they were laughing and kidding one another. Again, I was seen as some type of burden. They were joking about who was going to "take" me. One of them said: "Why don't you go with the Mexican," who was evidently a member of their group and perhaps the butt of jokes, and they all laughed. One person stepped forward, evidently the Mexican. I saw his face generally, but began to return before I could note any specific details of his appearance. This particular excursion didn't seem to yield anything dramatic. I was actually a bit surprised by the almost arbitrary nature of the encounter.

A few days later I decided to smoke again. This time the encounter was decidedly more involved. After rushing upward, I found myself among a crowd of people at some sort of ceremony, where certain ones were being chosen in the midst of some type of ecstatic regal atmosphere. I was given to understand, repeatedly, at the beginning of my encounter and later toward the end, that those like me, visitors to this realm of the dead, were representatives of a group of people not unlike a tribe or clan. It seemed as though at one point I was asked, in effect, what group I was representing, and I indicated that I was by myself and represented no group. This was not received favorably by my interrogators, and I was, in effect, brushed aside. The regal ceremony continued.

I was looking up to my left and there was a sort of platform, almost resembling a stage, seemingly covered with a white cloth. The whole plateau was bathed in bright yellow light. A woman, possibly black, was the mistress of ceremonies. She seemed to evince a very eminent and powerful demeanor. She was evidently choosing from among the crowd, which included both the newly dead and the representatives, including myself, for some type of honor, or the bestowal of some type of gift. At one point, she looked down and asked something to the effect of, "Are you the ones who died bravely" or "I'm looking for the ones . . ." I backed away indicating I wasn't among the ones she sought. As I did, I noticed a group of what appeared to be Mexicans, not dissimilar to the group of four or five men I'd encountered a few days before. I had the impression that these were indeed the ones she'd been looking for. They were evidently about to be taken up onto the platform and somehow rewarded—seemingly by being transported deeper into the ecstatic yellow light. I mean to make no representation that the group of Mexicans that were chosen was the same group I'd encountered in my previous session. At the same time, the coincidence of encountering a group of four or five Mexican men on two successive trials was interesting.

At that point, I began to almost tumble downward; at the same time, it became apparent that I was not alone, but others, apparently those who were also not chosen, accompanied me in what might be characterized as a symbolic fall from grace. This had the feeling of something akin to a game or ritual that is repeated in some sort of ceremonial fashion. Those who accompanied me were singing a song that was a repetitive sequence of perhaps five or six notes that I was given to understand was part of this ceremony. It almost felt reminiscent of a South Seas island chant accompanying a ritual that was an integral part of a tribal culture.

It seemed as though it was at this time that the assertion was repeated that those in my position represent a group and, in effect, go to death (or, more specifically, to the land of the dead) for their group to seek some type of communal benefit.

The song lasted long enough and was clear enough that I was able to isolate it to some extent and analyze it, noting its simplicity, repetitive nature, and other characteristics. It was not what one would term beautiful by any means, but more of a ceremonial chant that was used to somehow complete the ritual. It seemed, however, an interesting development to have the opportunity of hearing and analyzing a definite melody from such an exceptional source.

Again, although this particular session was extraordinarily vivid and concise, and clearly articulated specific concepts and premises, to speculate about any additional meaning or context would be pointless and presumptive. Salvia has the unique ability to present scenes and images in their own context, which is as succinct and complete as it is unfathomable.

5
SUBSIDIARY
OCCURRENCES

One of the fascinating aspects of salvia is that it can open the door to a variety of allied states of awareness. One such state that I found particularly intriguing was what I came to refer to in my notes as the "shrinking of the self." This state made its presence known under a variety of circumstances. It usually occurred in the afterglow state, following the normal deep trance. It has also occurred on a few occasions after smoking a less potent variety of crushed leaves.

The fact that I found particularly remarkable was that this state of shrinking of the self was not specific to the ingestion of salvia but is actually a normally occurring modification of human awareness. I had experienced this state numerous times, most often in childhood, usually after partially awakening from a deep sleep or at the point that just preceded sleep. This state was characterized by an altered sense of body image. The sense of scale was disturbed. I would feel "big" and "small" at the same time.

Simultaneously, the habitual reference points of up/down or right/left, for example, would be eclipsed by an overwhelming perception of "inner" and "outer." This would always be a novel event and was intriguing on many levels, since it entailed both somatic and psychological components. Unfortunately, its proximity to sleep would be its undoing, and any awareness I enjoyed would slowly slip away. I never thought much about this strange fleeting feeling, presuming it was simply an odd type of dream. With salvia, however, this state was to make its appearance once again in a relaxed and decidedly more conscious environment.

On one occasion, after smoking a bowl of weak, locally grown salvia as an experiment, I was initially disappointed in the fact that the normal intensity of the trance had not been achieved. After a few moments, however, I began to experience, quite unexpectedly, that same disorientation of body image that I'd experienced as a child. This time, however, the intensity of the experience was profoundly magnified; moreover, my awareness now was totally intact and concentrated to finally observe all the nuances of this heightened state.

In the months that followed, I would find this state occurring almost randomly, three or four times. Its intensity was such that it was becoming increasingly unpleasant, and I all but dreaded its appearance. This small cluster of occurrences, as it turns out, was almost an anomaly. I've only rarely experienced it subsequently and, even then, in varying degrees of intensity. Perhaps it could be "courted" in some manner and make its return—but, at any rate, has not manifested often of its own accord.

While this state was occurring regularly, I had the leisure to analyze my perceptions in depth. It reinforced the rather obvious fact that perhaps the most crucial element defining our general worldview, indeed our concept of reality itself, is the perception of our own physical body. Normally we perceive ourselves in the same manner. We look down through our eyes and see our arms and legs. We feel the sensations associated with our limbs, torso, and other body parts. We feel the touch of the chair on our back—our feet resting on the floor beneath us. We feel a comforting sense of scale. The floor is a few feet down. Our hand is perhaps a foot away holding the pen. This sense of scale is necessary to function in our physical body. We feel ourselves "in" our body. To walk, we simply use the muscles in our legs and back to stand up and walk across the room. When we stand, we find ourselves at the normal height to which we are accustomed. This combination of perception and three-dimensional movement in space solidifies our body image and our sense of scale.

This is necessary for survival. One needs to be able to

move in a comfortable environment to stay alive. This is the most important sensory integration that we learn as infants. We learn about three-dimensional space itself through the use of our body and the movement of our body through space. This conglomerate of perceptions is the determining factor in our view of the world. This is what makes the world "real." The world is out there, and we are inside our bodies—moving our limbs at will and maneuvering through what's out there.

If we analyze the body image itself, we generally feel and sense that we reside in the head—specifically, in what we've learned to call the brain—even though, of course, we have no direct experience of our brain through any senses. We experience this as the seat of consciousness. We feel that we are in the head, behind the eyes—that the eyes are our windows out on the external world. When we stand, we tell the muscles in our legs to contract; we tell the muscles in our torso to propel us forward onto those limbs. We stand and look down from the vantage point of our head. Our sense of self is dependent on this habitual complex of perceptions.

There is, however, another complex of perceptions that can be reached and can radically alter the entire worldview as described above.

Instead of perceiving ourselves in scale, it is possible, both naturally and plant induced, to perceive ourselves in a different light.

Under certain conditions of repose, accompanied by lack of external reinforcers and a continuation and concentration of awareness, the sense of self to which we're so accustomed can gradually become more concentrated and precise. It can begin to, in effect, withdraw from the external. The emphasis begins to shift from focusing on what we would normally consider outer elements to more abstract inner elements. As this process progresses in intensity, the normal sense of scale can begin to imperceptibly evaporate, as a new sense of scale begins to predominate. Whereas formerly we saw our body as "in here" and the world as "out there," we now, by degrees, begin to see our own physical body as "out there."

This is a gradual process in which we feel concentrated in the mind. We're deep within the mind—increasingly; the head and face begin to be viewed as more and more distant, assuming the form of a remote shell. As this sense of self continues to concentrate and withdraw into itself, the body is seen to be immense; the limbs immeasurably distant, seemingly miles long. The arms become huge, heavy contrivances that grow larger and more unreachable. The idea that one could move such an enormous apparatus by the force of one's will seems an absurdity.

As the shrinking of the self continues, the body becomes an infinite universe that becomes less differentiated. The concept of arms or legs has gradually vanished. There remains only the immensity of an increasingly formless universe that recedes more and more into the distance.

The self, on the other hand, is becoming more and more concentrated and, like sunlight through a magnifying glass, is becoming more precise and palpable. Not only is the perception of the self concentrating, but it seems as though awareness itself is becoming more intense and functional. The self has been reduced to a grain of sand in the immense ocean of the body.

As the self becomes more concentrated, all perceptions seem to surround it. The immense universe of the body has become spherical, with the minute grain of self at its innermost core. There is no up or down anymore. No right or left. There is only in and out. The self has become a magnificently precise point in space surrounded by the distant sphere of bodily perceptions.

Other gradations of this alteration of perception reinforce this distinction of the perceiver from the perceived. This centering of the self, it seems, can take various forms as one begins to descend into normal awareness. From my notes:

Upon returning, I was in a very deep state and felt that I'd gone very far. I felt as though I'd been taken out of my body and returned. As I came into normal awareness, I had a very strong sensation of shrinking of the self. This sensation consisted of feeling as though "I" consisted of a rod or channel that ran vertically below my "mind." My physical body was only peripherally connected to this self. The physical was an addendum or a footnote to this central awareness. Although I was gradually becoming more aware of my ordinary surroundings, this clear, central perception was paramount.

To characterize this awareness as "inner" is not wholly accurate. It was as if this "channel" was my real "body"; my primary perceptual reference was this elongated "self." It seemed as if this is always the real body, but due to a perceptual "mistake," the normal physical body is taken as real.

The real self does not have arms or legs, only a central awareness. This awareness, however, does have perceptions of that which is "outside" of itself. One of the areas outside itself, that it can choose to perceive, is the complex of perceptions that arises through a physical body. It can also choose, under certain circumstances, to not experience those perceptions and can withdraw, the way a hand is withdrawn from a glove. Our characteristic miscalculation is that we perceive ourselves as the glove, rather than the owner of the hand.

It seems that if this state of shrinking of the self could be maintained, deepened, and entered at will, a whole new perceptual matrix would emerge.

And on another occasion:

———

Concurrent with these sensations was another experiencing, but of a more psychological nature. This same experience had been noted in the past few salvia sessions.

This sensation consisted in an unbroken awareness on entering and traversing the salviaic landscape. As the trance began to recede, this unbroken continuity persisted, presenting as a feeling of pure vigilant awareness coupled with an alternate awareness of a state that was similar to, if not identical with, normal sleep. This dual awareness of vigilance and sleep manifested as perception of an inner and outer aspect of awareness. It was as if the inner vigilant self was cloaked in a mantle of restful sleep, yet functioned independently.

The awareness was full, concentrated, and augmented—with no danger of cessation (as with normal sleep)—the outer shell was slowly and restfully receding into sleep.

———

This shrinking of the self, although distinct from the general salviaic trance, seems to offer a valuable insight into that world, both inner and outer, that we regard as real. Like so many aspects of salvia, it inevitably leads one, in a very real way, to examine the nature of what we would tend to call the self and its relation to the outer world. One is left with the conclusion that the balance between the two is actually quite fluid and that, with the slightest nudge, the point of that balance can be shifted, leaving both concepts inexorably altered.

The effects of *Salvia divinorum* appear to be extremely variable from one person to another, and even for one person over the course of time. The experiences can be so disparate that it is hard to believe they could have originated from the same source. My attempts to chronicle my own experiences presuppose this subjective interpretation. I have no idea if the experiences of others might parallel my own or be of a radically different nature. Any attempt at comparison is compounded by the poverty of language to mirror the bizarre nature of the events in which one can find oneself immersed.

One such series of events in my own subjective case, that essentially eludes description, is a recurrent scenario that has often presented itself shortly after first entering the salviaic trance. After the rush of faces and feelings, there often appear scenes capturing people involved in seemingly mundane activities. These activities are, paradoxically, foreign yet familiar. Their apparently random nature belies their deceptively alien core. This involvement in activity is, in an indescribable way, linked with the almost imperceptible transformation of language. It's as if the activities portrayed can only be described in the dream language. They are somehow intrinsically linked, in the same way our ordinary language is linked, through nouns and verbs, to our sphere of activity. These actions that can be witnessed in the salviaic state, as well as in the transformative processes that permit their perception, are so subtle as to be virtually unnoticeable. They seem to take place almost under the threshold of awareness.

On many occasions, while beholding these alien activities, I would find myself in the unusual position of recognizing a group of actions as inexplicably familiar, yet being at a total loss as to their reason or purpose. The elements or objects that would be intrinsic to the unfolding scene, as well, would be foreign in form and function, yet comfortingly recognizable. A strange intuitive game would ensue within my mind each time such a vision would present itself. I would attempt to categorize the action, on some primitive, almost animal level, as something either familiar or foreign. Since the descriptors upon which we rely to solidify our perceptions were no longer within reach, the task would be all but impossible. Even concepts such as "familiar" or "foreign" can seem worlds away when immersed in the state.

For years, I thought that the events I was witnessing were ordinary human occurrences that were seemingly suddenly incomprehensible due to the rapid evaporation of thought and concept. After all, what else could they be? What other forms of human activity could exist? It would seem that any action of a genuinely foreign nature would have to be totally incomprehensible. As time went on, however, there was an unsettling jolt that would occur whenever these scenes would reemerge. I had no choice but to leave all the options open.

In one of my later experiences, I had the opportunity to observe a group of these scenes, as I'd done so often before. This time something was different. I had the distinct perception that the events that were unfolding before me were of an unmistakably foreign order. Although there were seemingly ordinary people involved in the execution of these tasks, the nature of the tasks themselves, as well as the elements involved in their completion, was totally alien to what we know. To maintain such a vision is virtually impossible, since the elements within oneself that could recognize it as foreign were, themselves, already rapidly dissolving. Imperceptibly, the actions that had seemed so incomprehensible a moment before begin to be recognizable in the new context in which one finds oneself immersed.

What these activities are is beyond the realm of comprehension. They seem to be so intrinsically connected to an essentially alien form of awareness that any attempt at rational understanding would seem futile. The fleeting duration of their perception only serves to reinforce their elusive nature. They do seem, however, to herald modifications of awareness that seem to be unfathomable and limitless.

In addition to the revelatory states described above, there are additional states in which one can find oneself that are seemingly barren and emotionally parched. Fortunately, these have been rare occurrences and are mentioned only for the sake of portraying the range of experience that salvia can engender.

In my own case, I had a series of sessions that might seem externally interesting due to the vividness of the visions, yet left me with a feeling of emptiness. This was due to the fact that, unlike other excursions, in these particular incidents I was not "taken." In the first instance, there were vague, almost arbitrary images that failed to command my attention. In one scene, I was being "presented" to an Inuit girl, but the situation was murky and lacked any emotional context. In a subsequent trial, I found myself in the company of three people—two men and a woman, evidently British, and seemingly well to do. They had a haughty demeanor and appeared to be conversing about their travels. I was distinctly aware of their conversation but was uninterested. There was nothing particularly likeable about these people, and the experience felt futile and dry.

At first I was unable to pinpoint what, exactly, was missing, but I knew something was wrong. I had never had such emotionally flat experiences before. For a few days, I had the horrifying thought that my benefactors had deserted me—that perhaps it was over and that my magical forays had ended. I feared that perhaps the portal that had opened for me had only been there for a limited time, and I had somehow failed to grasp that fact and act accordingly.

These dark thoughts, luckily, were put to rest with my next session. I was, once again, vigorously taken, and was, reassuringly, in the company of my hosts—in this case, a black woman who seemed to masterfully facilitate my release. It was only after this series of events that I understood that the process of being taken is, in fact, a seminal factor in the transformative process to which I'd become accustomed. The visions themselves seemed to be of a secondary nature, and although they define and articulate the various nuances of meaning at the core of the trance, the primary transportive mechanism is the plunging into this "state of presence" that catapults one so rapidly and so deeply into the other awareness.

As far as the cause of this series of hollow events, I have my suspicions. During this period, I would occasionally experiment with the oceanic inebriant kava kava. I would make an infusion of the dried root powder from the island of Vanuatu, or from Fiji, and consume the resultant liquid. The effects were a mild relaxing stimulation that would, before long, evolve into a natural dream-laden sleep. I had consumed kava the night before my barren episodes and suspected there might have been some correlation, chemical or otherwise. I've never read of any disharmony between salvia and kava; in fact, many people have consumed them together, but the coincidence was significant enough that I've since essentially abandoned kava, and the empty episodes have never returned.

In addition to the occasional fruitless events, other occurrences were almost unbearably intense. Again, these situations were very rare but should be relayed as a cautionary note, if nothing else. I've always tended to stay on the conservative side with salvia dosage, yet these types of experiences still presented themselves.

In the first event, I had obtained some 5X salvia extract from a new source and was interested in trying it and comparing the results with those to which I'd become accustomed. Erring on the side of caution, I used a very small amount, perhaps two-thirds my usual dose. I settled back in the chair and lit the pipe. Within seconds, I was propelled so deeply into the other side that I lost all touch with everything even vaguely familiar and felt sure that I was somehow being trapped—there being no trace of any avenue of return.

A sensation of panic ensued, and I opened my eyes, hoping to curtail the overwhelming rush of images and feelings that were rapidly engulfing me. I grabbed the arm of the chair, but my sense of touch was part of the vision—the chair blurring into a sea of viscous sensations. I stood up, but there was no up or down, only the swirl of foreign images and their constant tactile comprehension. Throughout this ordeal, there was a female personage with a mocking smile who seemed to say, "Go ahead, try it, but it won't work."

My next attempts led me to what I hoped would be the crisp edges of the door, the touch of which, frighteningly, also melted in a rubbery swirl. Evidently, I did, in fact, somehow make it outside and found myself surrounded by a surreal lunar landscape of moonlit snow. I began walking toward what I hoped was something familiar, and after what seemed like an eternity, I looked up and saw my car parked in front of the familiar silhouette of my house.

For the first time, I had the feeling that I would return, but it wasn't until another eternity had passed that I found myself walking into my living room—my wife's voice pulling me back into humanness. The entire event had lasted less than three minutes.

Looking back on the experience, I can't really say that I'd done anything wrong. I was cautious with the amount I'd smoked and only moved when my instinct for survival took over. I'd initially thought a sitter might have simply compounded the confusion, since the onset of the disorientation was so rapid and was of such an interior, tactile nature. In retrospect, however, a sitter might have provided some type of primitive physical assurance that could have rapidly restored some sense of equilibrium to the encounter. I suspect this particular extract might have either been mislabeled 10X or was perhaps extracted using different, more aggressive solvents. In any event, I was given a glimpse of a potentially more hostile environment that served to redouble my respect for the power that salvia can exercise on the psyche.

Strangely, aside from the numerous remarkable psychological nuances resulting from salvia, there is one that, although rare, should still be mentioned. That nuance is humor. As odd as it might seem, on several occasions, I've encountered decidedly humorous comments from this abstract destination.

On one occasion, just after smoking, I heard a female voice ask, "How would you like to wake up in a chair over here?"—the meaning, of course, being that I could awaken in that world, instead of this. The concept, although frightening in itself, was said in a joking, almost comforting way, implying that this wouldn't really be the case. The fact that the act of awakening in a chair was mentioned struck me as interesting, since it almost implied that I was being observed in this world. I would have thought that the boundary between the two realms could only be breached by a radical alteration of the psyche and not overstepped so readily by my companions.

Another incident took place while I was deep in the trance. I was accompanied by a group of people who were in the process of leaving where they were. They were preparing for travel. One young female asked jokingly, "What about Mr. Meat-in-the-Chair?" referring to my connection to my physical body as a hindrance to their movement. This particular appellation struck me as both succinct and hilarious, both at the time and again after returning. Although this idea took the form of humor, it merely reinforced the concept that I was almost a burden to my hosts and had to be cared for.

One other incident highlighted the mood of lightness that can occasionally appear. Again, this occurred just after smoking one pipeful. I was preparing to light the second pipe when I heard a voice comment, "Ooh, two pipes!" in a teasing manner, implying this would be too much for me. As before, this was said in a good-natured way and only served to strengthen my feelings of familiarity and affection with my escorts.

This again underscored the perception that I could be observed in the ordinary world with only the slightest brush with salvia.

6

REALITY
OF THE VISIONS

O ne of the primary questions that arises when
discussing salvia is the validity or reality of the
visions that one encounters. This issue is actually much more complex than it appears on the surface.
The nature of the visions is comprised of numerous levels
of articulation and involvement, within a series of sessions
for any one person. To compound the matter, everyone has
a unique subjective experience with salvia, which can differ
radically from that of someone else.

Notwithstanding these differences, the reality of the
visions must at one point, sooner or later, be addressed.

Ironically, in order for a genuine appraisal of these
visions to occur, a radical dissection of our ordinary perceptions is necessary. Of course, the simplest reaction,

particularly among those who are unfamiliar with salvia, would be to pronounce the visions as unreal. After all, they take place in an altered state of awareness and, therefore, are mere creations of the mind or imagination. They have no connection to the real, solid world that we perceive on a daily basis and which is our main frame of reference. The landscapes that might present themselves are not accessible in a controlled manner, where they can be rationally measured against the ruler of our ordinary perceptions.

Many people would feel that this is the only reasonable analysis—that no matter how real the visions might seem, they are the result of a chemical modification of the brain and, as such, can have no inherent reality. This is the "rational" approach (sure the visions might have some kind of inner, subconscious content that might even be useful for attaining some glimpse into the "recesses of the mind," but they ultimately spring from the mind itself).

The situation with which one is presented is not unlike a humorous story we've all heard. In the story, a man walking on the street at night encounters a companion searching the ground beneath a streetlight. When asked what he is looking for, he gestures behind him, into the darkness, replying, "I dropped my key over there and can't find it."

"But if you dropped your key over there, why are you looking for it over here?" asks his friend.

"Because the light is much better over here," he replies.

When attempting to determine the reality of the salviaic

visions, the first impulse is to examine the phenomenon where "the light is much better"—our normal awareness, based on thought and our habitual response to the sensory input that constructs and reinforces our world. Regrettably, just as in the story, this is not where the key is to be found. Since birth, we've been told consciously or unconsciously that our current sensory framework is the ultimate bench-mark of the entire cosmos. The science of astronomy, for instance, is based on this assumption. Anything outside that framework is called into question. The nature of the perceiver is never factored into the equation.

In an odd twist, however, it can be these very salviaic visions that can allow one to step back and analyze the nature of the instruments used in making such a scientific analy-sis. Perhaps the primary foundation of all science, which is so intrinsically entrenched as to be virtually invisible, is the unquestioned assumption that we, in actuality, perceive the real world. To imply that the world that we perceive on a day-to-day basis is a miscalculation or a false perception can, on the surface, seem ludicrous, yet if one were to sincerely analyze the components on which our worldview is based, the presumptive nature of our "rational" framework stands out in a less flattering light.

The obvious place to begin any examination would be the senses—after all, this is our only connection to the world. These five narrow conduits of information are the only way we have of assessing the infinite universe. Like the blind men and the elephant, each of the senses conveys its limited perceptions but, by their very nature, can never fully apprehend the real substance of the object under examination. It would seem crucial to understand that the world presented by the senses is intrinsically incomplete. The information gleaned from the scientific world itself demonstrates this. There are myriad forces surrounding and penetrating us—cosmic rays, infrared light, high-frequency sounds, and ultraviolet rays, for example, of which we have no perception. Even animals perceive a realm of perception that eludes us.

It seems logical to posit that there are other realms of perception that, although valid, are not open to us in our present state. If we were able to perceive such genuine information, which is now inaccessible due to the poverty of our senses, one must concede that the transmission of that information would, by its nature, have to present a foreign form. If we were to experience the sense of smell, for instance, for the first time, we can only imagine the foreignness of the experience. It would have to transform our entire view of the world. Things that had been inaccessible could suddenly and magically be sensed. We would know, for instance, of a distant campfire without having seen or felt it. If one perceives the world in a new way, it would seem these new perceptions must present as alien and indescribable.

The visions engendered by salvia are of a unique order

in that in some essential way they can articulate, with astounding precision, a relationship that could never have been imagined between the perceiver and the perceived. The characterization of the phenomenon as a vision can, itself, be misleading, since this seems to imply some sort of passive visual event. In reality, the salviaic visions are themselves almost a vehicle, a vessel for the transformative, what might be called "realizing" (in the sense of being made real) of the perceiver.

Salvia can allow us to, in effect, "step back" from our perceptions, as if they themselves were an external phenomenon. In such a state, it can become apparent that we do not witness the world as such but, in reality, witness our senses. At the same time, it becomes increasingly apparent that those same senses, in an internal sense, can perceive a much more fluid world than we have come to expect. The visions encountered begin to have not only an apparent reality but also a type of heightened validity that becomes more and more undeniable with repeated familiarity. This is not the realm of philosophical speculation but a life-and-death-like encounter of animal intensity. The thought that such experiences can later be dismissed by "rational" understanding is laughable.

Some years ago, after learning of the unique experiences that were possible, a friend of mine decided to try salvia. After smoking a good dose, his visions ensued. He found himself looking at a group of playing cards. At one point the faces in the cards "came to life" and were silently staring at him in a very serious manner. This terrified him, and he stood up, dispelling the vision. Although the form of the playing cards was abstract, almost allegorical, the experience of contact they engendered was, in my friend's eyes, frighteningly real. The form of the contact was of much less significance than the contact itself. To attempt to characterize such an experience using the old ruts of "real" and "unreal" is misguided, at best.

If one were to accept the posit that salvia can, under certain circumstances, engender a state of "thoughtless awareness," it follows that that state would, by its very nature, consist of perceptual elements that would be uniquely foreign to the realm of our ordinary experience. This cessation of thought, unlike the mere suspension of thought that can be achieved for a few moments at a time, is a steady state— a dramatic, alien, effortless release from mentation. This state can, understandably, afford one the opportunity to witness one's own perceptual and conceptual bias, in a way that is unparalleled. To attempt to define an experience that is beyond thought by thought itself is, like the quest for the key in the light, obviously doomed from the outset.

Culturally, we're conditioned to react in predictable ways to any incursion of the unknown. In our modern Western culture, the first reaction to any plant-induced visionary occurrence is to pronounce it a "creation of the mind." This relieves the pressure, since we've all been taught about the mind and feel we know, even if only generally, what it is. In reality, of course, we have no real understanding of what the mind is, but the term is a convenient attempt to categorize what is incomprehensible.

The mind "resides" in the brain, which is in the head, at the top of our body, the form of which is delivered by our senses. What could be simpler? If one perceives something or someone "outside," it is real. If that someone or something is perceived "inside," it is unreal. "A hair perhaps divides the false from true," as the Rubaiyat says. Whether the source of our perception is from within or without, however, begins to lose relevance with a substance like salvia that can essentially demonstrate, particularly through traversing the deeper levels of trance, that concepts such as "inner" and "outer" are relative perceptual miscalculations that we've come to accept. Salvia can begin to erode the dogmatic conceptual rigidity that prevents us from connecting with the mystery that surrounds us.

When comparing the salviaic visions to our normal world, the obvious distinction is the feeling that this world and its perceptions are solid and dependable; whereas, the perceptions offered by the salviaic state are fleeting and, from the vantage point of our normal awareness, bizarre and foreign. While in the salviaic trance, however, the discrepancies between these two states of awareness are less obvious. In our normal framework of awareness the perceiver goes unnoticed and therefore is never a factor for consideration. This is not necessarily the case with salviaic awareness.

The fact that the two states are intrinsically entwined can become apparent at the conclusion of the visionary state, as one gradually descends from the freedom of the abstract to the burden of description and the stricture of ordinary thought. At these times, the underpinnings of ordinary awareness can be glimpsed in a way that is all but incomprehensible from our normal viewpoint—a point at which the customary mode of awareness seems a tenuous construction that attains solidity gradually through a process, it seems, of a type of automatic "returning to form" and the weight of its own habit.

Despite the fact that this gradual descent is a welcome return from the alien abstraction bestowed by salvia, one can be left with the sense—and, of course, this is merely a subjective impression—that such a descent could be side-stepped in the event that one chose to relinquish that return. Whether or not this choice is solely within the purview of the moment of death, as it appears may occasionally be the case, is, of course, unknown. The ironic fact that emerges is that, no matter how real and solid one's perceptions of the world, they must always rely on a perceiver. And it's that perceiver that is fluid and formless. Strangely, solidity relies for its very foundation on the insubstantial.

The fact that our modern world is so separate from the visionary environment cultivated for millennia is the exception rather than the rule. Our "spiritual" life is based, most commonly, on "faith" in various descriptions provided by others, rather than on direct and transformative experience that can be surprisingly accessible. The bias against plant-augmented investigation helps to keep this absurd situation well entrenched.

When my own initial experiences began to allude to the land or place of the dead, I, myself, was skeptical. Aside from the fact that I thought such characterizations were simplistic generalizations, it just seemed too easy—almost predictable. Yet, as these scenarios kept recurring, and as their consistency was proving undeniable, I was gradually forced to reexamine my own prejudices. Repeated indications, as well as several distinct perceptual events—resulting in essentially new realms of experience—left me no choice but to accede to their validity.

Whether this land of the dead is a steady state or a transitional state—which all indications have tended to support—has yet to be discovered. Strangely, even now, in my ordinary state, to refer to such concepts as a place of the dead seems almost an absurdity and yet, when returning from the immediate fluid state of salviaic trance, it is this habitual, leaden awareness that emerges as the true absurdity—the arbitrary constrictive trap.

When considering this notion of a realm of the dead, one question that arises is whether or not it is possible to contact persons we knew who have passed away. On this point, I must admit that all options are open. From my own experiences thus far, I've not found this to be possible. In order to achieve that intensity, whereby this state is accessed, thought must be abandoned. When thought and memory are abandoned, it follows that our memories of friends and loved ones must also vanish.

The act of "attempting to remember" is rooted firmly in our ordinary mode of mentation and itself requires much thought and more or less rigid conceptualization. And yet, there have been times when I've felt a distinct, almost thoughtless archetypal remembrance of family members who have died, almost as if an ancient scent had momentarily wafted past. At other times, it's seemed as though certain realms of contact and affection superceded thought and were almost, on some level at any rate, intrinsic to one's nature. In general, though, it seems that to achieve the deeper states with salvia, one must, in effect, forget oneself and, in that forgetting, let go of one's ordinary thoughts and affections to whatever extent one is capable, with the understanding that if such contact is possible and does indeed occur, it is, in all probability, outside of our control.

Another point that should be addressed is the reality of the people encountered in the salviaic trance. Our ordinary reason would posit that such encounters are no different from those of dreams and, as such, have no intrinsic reality. This, of course, is a very valid point.

Again, we view those people in our ordinary sense-based world as real, all others as unreal. If we examine our experience more closely, we find that we attribute awareness to beings outside ourselves based on our sensory input. There can be no other gauge to intuit external awareness. Aside from the external indicators of movement, communication, and so forth, we have no real proof that awareness is present in other beings.

When considering the beings encountered in the salviaic state, one must, inevitably, use the same criteria. We can only intuit awareness based on sensory input. If we can, in effect, engage in conscious communication there, and sense the reality of our companions as strongly as we sense the reality of our companions in our normal sphere, the only challenge to their validity comes from our ordinary thoughts and habitual conceptualizations. Again, the concepts of real and unreal are thoughts that have meaning only in the narrow confines of our day-to-day awareness. In the fluid darkness of the trance, there is only experience.

It would appear that if we are able to feel and touch another realm with the same senses with which we feel and touch this world, then the same criteria should apply— either the sensory world perceived through salvia has some claim to validity, or our perceptual assessment of this world is fatally flawed.

Probably the single most important change in perception that salvia can grant is the understanding of the difference between thought and awareness. In most Western cultures, it would seem, these two facets of our psyche are seen as one; yet the distinction between the two can't be overemphasized. Awareness is a silent steady state of what might be called self-acknowledgment. It is a raw, unfettered, perceptual equilibrium.

Thought, on the other hand, takes work. One must remember and maintain scores of concepts, buttressed by myriad words, to retain and connect, it seems, even the simplest of thoughts. This gives rise to a familiar sense of solidity and cohesiveness that can be both liberating and restrictive. Liberating in that we have the power to describe, weigh, and compare the elements of our world; restrictive, in that our world begins to consist only of those elements that can be described, weighed, and compared. Salvia can restore, if only for a few moments, our birthright of pure thoughtless awareness that lies quietly beneath the clatter of thought.

Ultimately, it seems, without some type of direct experience of the transformative nature of substances such as salvia, shedding light on the genuine fallacy of the validity of our normal perceptions and revealing hints about the true nature of the perceiver, any differentiation of the real from the false will remain in the realm of words alone.

EPILOGUE

Any writings hoping to chronicle the exploration of a substance as remarkable and complex as salvia must be seen as a continuing process. In a work such as this there is no end point, no conclusion. One can only hope to delineate a certain sequence of experiences, within a defined time frame. At some point a choice must be made to begin that framing process with a given number of events.

My aim has been to highlight those significant occurrences that took place within that window. Over the course of five years, certain consistencies have made themselves manifest in the experiences elaborated through salvia. It is this group of perceptual and experiential benchmarks that defined the uniqueness of the salviaic experience. To continue delineating this same perceptual framework with additional experiential entries would seem redundant.

It seems as though salvia can lead to a certain type of abstract threshold. At some point one must choose to cross or abandon that threshold. I have endeavored to describe the topography, as I've witnessed it, leading up to that boundary. To cross over would entail, it seems, a complete immersion in the unknown to such a depth as would be virtually limitless.

In my own case, if such a crossing should occur, the results, I would think, would be as indescribable as they were intensely personal. Either quality, it would seem, would preclude recounting. Anecdotal accounts, after a period of time, would seem to serve no purpose, since salvia itself yields its secrets so directly and completely.

During the compilation of these notes, salvia was a legal hallucinogen throughout the United States and much of the world. In the last few years, the situation has begun to change. Shamanic exploration through the use of salvia is now illegal in quite a few countries and extending to many states in the United States. Before long, any such exploration will, no doubt, be viewed as a criminal pursuit.

It seems an unflattering snapshot of the modern Western psyche that the elusive treasure retrieved more than forty years ago by two men who ventured into the Mexican mountains has been discarded in such an ignorant, tragic way.

For those who may choose to investigate the landscape

opened through salvia, I can only echo a fragment of a curandero's prayer:

> *Lord (Saint Peter) attend him*
> *That he may see the Universe*
> *What there is in the world*
> *Everything*
> *Help him, raise him*
> *May he see what there is*
> *All that he wishes to know*
> *Save him, care for him*

INDEX

5X, 22, 60, 73–74, 110

African village, 42
animate corpses, 59–60
awareness, 47
  cumulative, 16–17
  expansion of, 2
  thought and, 125
  thoughtless, 29, 80–81, 119
  two worlds and, 80–81
  vigilance and sleep, 104
  See also language; shrinking of
    self

birth, 70
bliss, 20, 58, 68
Bunnell, Sterling, 2
burden, author as, 32, 93, 113

Caribbean environment,
  84–85
cartoons, 13, 14, 64–65

cat's cradle, 29
ceremonies, 2, 37, 93–95
channel, body as, 103
chants, 95
cocoon, experience in, 72, 82
communication, 50–51, 64–65,
  72, 75–77
contact, 87–88, 119, 122–23
continuity, 16–17
corpses, 59–60
crown chakra, 20
curanderos, 2

darkness, 10
dead, land of the, 32–34, 55–56,
  122–23
death, 58–59, 66–67
  fear of, 79–80
  joy and, 91–92
deliriant, salvia as, 14
direction, 19–20
divination, 2, 35–37

DMT, 9
dolphinlike beings, 21
dosage, 9, 110
dream body, 90
dream language, 53–54, 55–56
dreams, 54–55
dream time, 39
drumming, 87

emotions. *See* feelings
emptiness, 108–9
entrapment, 87
eternity, 39
extract, 110, 111–12
extraction, 8–9

faith, 2, 71, 122
familial connections, 55–56, 64,
    88
fear of death, 79–80
feelings, 18, 31, 55
flesh, blissful death, 59
flesh of the gods, 68–69
freshness, 57–58
functional awareness, 29

gifts, 68, 90–91, 94

Haitian village, 42
hall, experience in, 70–71
hallucinogens, 1–3, 14
higher physics, 88
Hofmann, Albert, 1–2

humanness, 66, 71, 86, 111
humor, 112–13

ingesting, methods of, 8–10
insectlike beings, 72
intoxication, 44
isolation, 10. *See also* solitude
itching, 58

Jamaican woman, 86

kava kava, 109–10
kinship, 55–56, 68

land of the dead, 32–34, 55–56,
    122–23
language, 41, 49–53, 56, 71–72,
    105–6
LSD, 16

madness, 16, 17, 63
Mazatecan leaf, 45, 67
Mazatecs, 1–2, 7
McClure, Michael, 2
melody, 95–96
memory, 26–27, 33, 39–40, 50,
    54, 56, 63
mentation, 35, 119, 123
Mexican people, 26–27, 75,
    92–93, 94
mind, 119–20
morning glory seeds. *See*
    Ololiuqui